Scenic Driving

WEST VIRGINIA

Help Us Keep This Guide Up to Date

Every effort has been made by the author and editors to make this guide as accurate and useful as possible. However, many things can change after a guide is published—trails are rerouted, regulations change, techniques evolve, facilities come under new management, etc.

We would love to hear from you concerning your experiences with this guide and how you feel it could be improved and kept up to date. While we may not be able to respond to all comments and suggestions, we'll take them to heart and we'll also make certain to share them with the author. Please send your comments and suggestions to the following address:

The Globe Pequot Press
Reader Response/Editorial Department
P.O. Box 480
Guilford, CT 06437

Or you may e-mail us at:

editorial@globe-pequot.com

Thanks for your input, and happy travels!

Scenic Driving

WEST VIRGINIA

BRUCE SLOANE

FALCON®

GUILFORD, CONNECTICUT

An imprint of The Globe Pequot Press

Cover: The New River Gorge Bridge, West Virginia.
Photo credits: All photos are by the author unless otherwise noted.
Maps: Tony Moore

Library of Congress Cataloging-in-Publication Data is available.

ISBN 0-7627-1137-X

Manufactured in the United States of America
First Edition/Second Printing

contents

THE SCENIC DRIVES

acknowledgments

Without the help of West Virginia's friendly people, my travels—and yours—would not have been so interesting, fun, and informative. It's impossible to list everyone, but here are a few folks who have been especially helpful. My thanks go out to you, and may you continue to enrich the lives of future visitors.

Heartfelt thanks go to the West Virginia Division of Tourism, particularly Cindy Harrington and Caryn Gresham, who helped get this project on the road, provided signposts along the way, and made sure the signposts were accurate. Their review of the manuscript has helped make this book more accurate and helpful to readers and motorists.

Thanks also to Randolph Deloatch of Kimball, local politician and statesman, who is doing more than his share to preserve West Virginia's heritage and build an economy based on sustainable resources. All politics may be local, but the results can be global. To Ashby Berkley of Pence Springs, a West Virginia native who proved you can go home again. Thanks also go to Eleanor Mailloux of Helvetia for delicious dining and delightful conversation, but mostly for keeping the old traditions alive. And to Jeff Lipscomb of Charles Town for his fond memories of a West Virginia childhood.

Thanks also flow to the Monroe County Byways Committee for their marvelous booklet on Monroe's most scenic drives, to Fred B. Lewis of the Wells Inn, Sistersville, and to Jackie Stocker, Lakes Region resident.

I am also indebted to executive editor Mary Luders at The Globe Pequot Press, who knows how to soothe edgy authors. Last, but far from least, my thanks go to my traveling partner, navigator, driver, organizer, map maker, critic, and wife: Thank you, Joy, for being with me on the road, at home, and in between.

introduction

West Virginia! No other state has such a mystique. It's a small state, forty-first in size, but within its 24,000 square miles you can find high tech coal mines, rock ridges, isolated valleys, sophisticated cities, scenic railroad rides, roaring rivers and white water rafting, canyons and gorges, the Hatfields and McCoys, rock climbing, ancient Indian mounds, Civil War sites, winding roads, ski resorts, historical buildings, fishing streams, arctic plants, caves and underground streams, steel mills, forests, hunting, mountain vistas—the list could go on and on. West Virginia also has proud and friendly people; people who love their state and take pride in their heritage; people happy to live where they are, and happy, too, to show you why they love their land.

The state is divided into two physiographic provinces. The western two-thirds lies in the Appalachian Plateau province of relatively flat-lying rocks with mineable coal. This area is severely dissected by streams into a maze of irregular hills and valleys. West Virginia is the only state to lie almost entirely within the Appalachian Plateau.

The eastern third of the state is dominated by the northeast-southwest ridges of the Valley and Ridge province, with its intricately folded rocks, sinuous peaks, and cavernous valleys. An exception is the extreme portion of the Eastern Panhandle near Harpers Ferry, which is an extension of the Blue Ridge Mountains and Shenandoah Valley of Virginia.

The boundary between the Valley and Ridge province and the Appalachian Plateau is the imposing Allegheny Front, which at its maximum rises 2,500 feet above the plateau and includes the highest and some of the most scenic areas of the state.

Eroded into a thousand-foot-deep gorge across the Allegheny Front and much of the state is the New River, known, along with the Gauley and Cheat Rivers, for world-class white-water rafting.

The southern and southwest areas of the state contain some of the largest deposits of bituminous coal in the country. Mining practices during the early 1900s scarred the land in many places. In recent years reclamation projects have helped partially restore some damaged areas. In addition to bituminous coal, the state's economic mineral deposits are abundant oil and gas, limestone,

The New River roars along 1,000 feet below in Grandview State Park.

sandstone, and rock-salt beds. As mining has become more mechanized, jobs have grown scarce, and gradually recreation and travel are being recognized as employment possibilities and as the best use that can be made of the land.

The Ohio River forms most of the western border of the state and has been an important avenue for transportation since the first settlers. Industrial sites are common along the Ohio, but the river retains much of its former charm.

The 2000 census shows a population of 1.8 million happy residents (and a few soreheads), an increase of less than 1 percent from 1990. Charleston, the state capital, with 53,000 people is the largest city; the Charleston metropolitan area has a population of about 200,000.

The census shows a movement to rural and country living because most larger cities and towns lost population while the rural population increased. The biggest increase was in the Eastern Panhandle, within commuting distance of the high tech and government jobs of northern Virginia east of Harpers Ferry.

Forests cover about three-fourths of the state, and there are approximately 2,000 miles of streams and rivers. The state's highest point is Spruce Knob with an elevation of 4,863 feet; the lowest point is the Potomac River at Harpers Ferry with an elevation of 247 feet.

At lower elevations the forests consist of red and white oak, hickory, yellow poplar, maple, black cherry, and other hardwoods. At higher elevations and on steep slopes and gorges are several species of pines, hemlock, and spruce. Logging is widespread and an important economic factor.

Virginia white-tailed deer, rabbit, squirrel, skunk, raccoon, opossum, and groundhog are common, and, in high country, black bear. Streams support smallmouth and largemouth bass, trout, and pike; larger rivers have perch, bluegill, catfish, and other species. Hunting and fishing are both popular recreational activities. The many varied habitats lead to abundant bird life, with more than 500 species known in the state.

The earliest inhabitants of the area were the Adena or Mound Builder Indians. They were followed by the Hopewell people, who in turn were succeeded by the Iroquois and Cherokee in the seventeenth century. Around 1730 the first permanent white settlers came to the area. After the American Revolution the state was part of Virginia, but in 1861 the population voted against secession and West Virginia was admitted as a separate state in 1863.

Most of the state enjoys four distinct seasons but with a wide range because of the great variation in terrain. Precipitation averages 40 to 60 inches across the state. Snowfall averages 20 to 30 inches per year, except in the high Canaan Valley and mountain areas, which receive 160 to 180 inches annually.

The Fish Creek Covered Bridge in Hundred.

The scenic drives in this book cover all sections of the state and were selected to display the most interesting scenic, historical, and unique features. The drives are described from a starting point to an end point, or from a starting point in a loop back to the starting point. You can begin most drives at several places along the route, or tour them in reverse order. Most are over paved, two-lane roads. A few drives or sections of them are over rough, unpaved roads; these are clearly explained to help you decide if you want to travel there.

Some drives should not be attempted in winter, or at any time if inclement weather is expected. Many attractions are not open during the winter months, so be sure to check out the ones you are interested in before leaving.

Information for each drive starts with a **General description,** which gives you a one-paragraph thumbnail sketch of the drive, including total mileage. **Special attractions** lists some of the main points of the drive. These can be scenic, historical, cultural, or just plain interesting. **Location** gives the general location within the state and the nearest large town (if there is one).

The old church at the Swiss town of Helvetia.

West Virginia has more than 2,000 miles of flowing streams.

Driving route numbers and name lists the route numbers on the drive in the following format:

- I   Interstate highway. I–79, for example. No drives follow interstates, but some drives begin at interstate exits, or an interstate is mentioned as a reference point.
- US   United States highway, such as US 119 and US 220.
- WV   West Virginia highway, for instance WV 28, WV 5–1, or WV 28/55. If the road has a name, that is shown also. Some roads change route numbers when they cross county lines. Dashes (–) indicate feeder roads (WV 5-1, WV 28-1). Slashes (/) indicate multiple route numbers for the same stretch of highway (WV 28/55).
- FS   U.S. Forest Service Route, FS 11 for example.

Some drives are especially attractive when spring wildflowers or fall colors are present. Other drives cannot be made in winter or should not be attempted at that time of year. **Travel season** shows this information. However, even though a drive is listed as all season, some attractions do not operate all year round. **Camping** lists public and private campgrounds along the route and nearby. "Complete facilities" indicates that at least some sites have hookups, water, and indoor plumbing. **Services** refer to the availability of gasoline, food, and lodging along the drive. "All services" means that all three are readily obtainable. **Nearby attractions** lists points of interest near the drive, including other scenic drives.

It's only a slight exaggeration to say that every road in West Virginia is a scenic drive. Even the interstates are beautiful, and every road in the Monongahela, George Washington, and Jefferson National Forests is a scenic road. For some non–interstate roads along major highways that are not included in this book, try these: US 33 between Bridgeport and Parkersburg, US 119 from Charleston to the Kentucky line, or any part of US 219 (parts of it are already on scenic drives). Explore on your own, and happy driving!

The Appendix lists phone numbers, addresses, Web sites, and e-mail addresses of visitor information centers and local points of interest, arranged numerically by drive number.

West Virginia

LOCATOR MAP

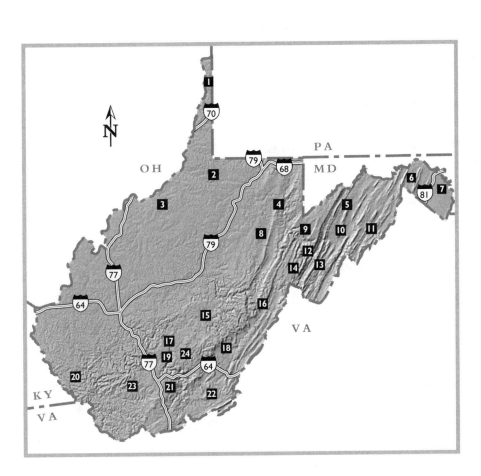

LEGEND

Scenic Drive - paved	▬▬▬▬▬	River	∿
Scenic Drive - unpaved	▪▪▪▪▪▪▪▪▪	Lake	⬭
Interstate Highway	═══	Peak	⛰
Other Roads	═══	Campground	Λ
Interstate	77	Point of Interest	■
U.S. Highway	50 250	Town	O Riverton
State and County Routes	150		
Forest Road	112	Scenic Drive Location	WEST VIRGINIA
Trail	▪-▪-▪-▪-		
Railroad	+++++++++		
State Line	▬ - ▬ - ▬	Orientation	N↑
National Forest Boundary	— — — —	Scale	0 5 10 Miles
State Park Boundary	▭▭▭▭		

Northern Panhandle

THE INDUSTRIAL OHIO RIVER

GENERAL DESCRIPTION: A 55-mile drive along the Ohio River bluffs in the Northern Panhandle of the state, with forays to the wooded uplands away from the river, ending in Wheeling.

SPECIAL ATTRACTIONS: The Ohio River, Mountaineer Gaming Resort, Tomlinson Run State Park, glass factory tours, Bethany College, Oglebay Resort and Conference Center, Victorian Wheeling, and Wheeling Downs Race Track.

LOCATION: Northernmost West Virginia.

DRIVING ROUTE NUMBERS AND NAME: WV 2, 3, 8, 67, 88, 208; OH 7 for the complete loop.

TRAVEL SEASON: All year. Travel is very heavy in November and December during Wheeling's Festival of Light.

CAMPING: Tomlinson Run State Park has fifty-four campsites, most with complete facilities, and a Rent-A-Camp program for novice campers.

SERVICES: All services are available in many towns along the drive.

NEARBY ATTRACTIONS: Grave Creek Mound Historic Site, Old West Virginia Penitentiary, and the Palace of Gold (these are all on Drive 2); Pittsburgh, Pennsylvania (40 miles east), Hillcrest Wildlife Management Area, and Castleman Run Lake Wildlife Management Area.

THE DRIVE

West Virginia's narrow Northern Panhandle juts north from the rest of the state, bordered by Ohio and the Ohio River on the west and Pennsylvania on the east. The only section of the state north of the Mason-Dixon Line, parts of it are less than 40 miles from Pittsburgh, and its northernmost point is closer to Canada than it is to the southern border of West Virginia.

The Ohio River has been a transportation artery and major influence in the area for more than 200 years. From its beginning at the confluence of the Allegheny and Monongahela Rivers in Pittsburgh, Pennsylvania, the Ohio

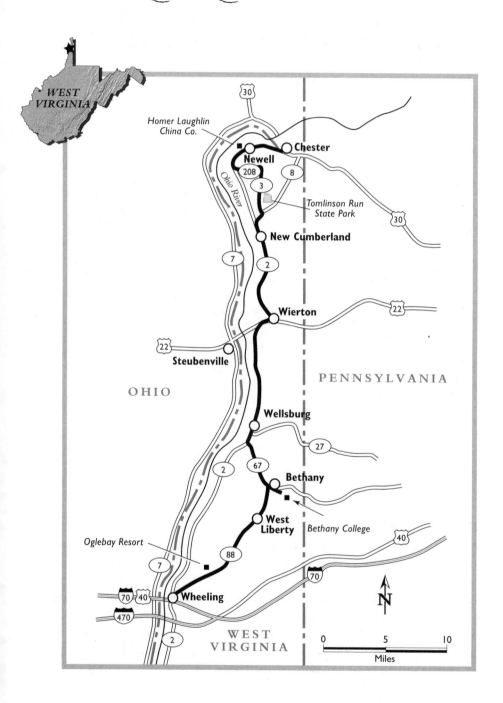

WEST VIRGINIA

30

Homer Laughlin
China Co.

Chester

Newell

208

8

3

Tomlinson Run
State Park

30

New Cumberland

Ohio River

7

2

Wierton

22

22

Steubenville

PENNSYLVANIA

OHIO

Wellsburg

27

2

67

Bethany

West
Liberty

Bethany College

40

Oglebay Resort

7

88

70

70

40

Wheeling

N

470

2

WEST
VIRGINIA

0   5   10

Miles

River flows for 981 miles through several Midwest states before merging into the Mississippi River near Cairo, Illinois. For about 250 miles the Ohio River is shared by Ohio and West Virginia, marking the western boundary of West Virginia.

This drive follows the Ohio River from the northern tip of West Virginia south to Wheeling. Drive 3 also follows the Ohio, from New Martinsville to Parkersburg.

Before the Pleistocene ice sheets, the preglacial Ohio River flowed north to empty into the ancestral Great Lakes. Several times during the Pleistocene epoch, continental glaciers formed large lakes to the north, damming the Ohio. With this outlet blocked the river began flowing south, eventually reaching the Gulf of Mexico. As the climate warmed and the glacial ice melted, torrents of water filled the Ohio River, swelling it to many times its present size. The river continued to maintain this drainage pattern along its present course after the ice sheets melted.

The Ohio is a working river. Steel mills, coal mines, power companies, and manufacturing plants line its banks or lie nearby. Transporters—specialized aerial conveyer belts—carry coal from mineheads, often several miles away in the surrounding hills, down to the river. There they are loaded onto mile-long barges pushed by powerful diesel tow boats that slowly work their way up and down the waterway.

The Ohio is also a scenic river. A thousand feet to half a mile wide here, its long and wide curves flow between banks of verdant hills that rise steeply several hundred feet above the river, in places accentuated by rocky cliffs of sandstone and limestone. The fertile fields adjacent to the river support herds of cattle. Occasional towns, large and small, huddle close to the river or spread out along the wider level areas. Graceful bridges, some new, some more than 150 years old, span the water.

In the 1700s the Ohio River was used by explorers and settlers traveling west. Towns and commerce flourished along the river while most of the surrounding territory was an almost unknown wilderness. Local boatyards used the abundant timber to construct boats for the westward migration down the Ohio; farmers and traders shipped their goods downriver on a one-way trip to New Orleans, where the boats were dismantled for their lumber.

Travel was restricted by the depth of the water, which during dry months was less than 1 foot between Pittsburgh and Cincinnati. Many shippers had to wait, sometimes months, for rains and high water before sending their products downriver.

In the early 1800s the federal government began to clear and maintain the channel, but navigation was still difficult and treacherous. After the rail line from the Atlantic Ocean to the Ohio River was completed in 1852, the demand for better river transportation increased, but it wasn't until 1885 that the first lock and dam was opened, creating a navigable pool of water just below Pittsburgh. Today fifty-three dams and sets of locks straddle the Ohio River between Pittsburgh and Cairo, Illinois. These provide year-round waterway travel in a series of stages up and down the 460-foot difference in river elevation between Pittsburgh and the upper Mississippi River.

You can make this a loop drive by crossing the river in Wheeling and following OH 7 north. (This solves the problem of how to get to Chester to begin the actual drive.) OH 7 is a four-lane highway along the west bank (Ohio side) of the Ohio River with many scenic views of the river and the West Virginia shoreline. At East Liverpool follow US 30 south across the river to Chester to WV 2 and turn south for the main drive. This adds about 45 miles to the drive, for a total of about 100 miles.

THE WORLD'S LARGEST TEAPOT

The West Virginia portion of the drive begins in Chester at the intersection of WV 2 and US 30 near the World's Largest Teapot. Follow two-lane WV 2 south along the bluffs of the Ohio River, passing numerous bridges that cross the river to East Liverpool, Ohio.

A few miles past Chester, the drive passes the well-marked entrance to the Homer Laughlin China Company, the main industry in Newell. The company's popular, low-cost, multihued Fiesta chinaware is used daily in millions of homes and restaurants. A retail store is open daily; factory tours are conducted several times a week.

West Virginia has been a major glass-producing state since the early 1800s. Glass manufacturing requires abundant supplies of silica, SiO_2. The source of the silica comes not from beaches, but from sandstone rock—fossil beaches— and for high-grade glass manufacturing it must be pure, at least 96 percent silica. The Oriskany sandstone, found abundantly throughout the state, meets this requirement. Today the only major quarry for Oriskany sand is near Berkeley in the Eastern Panhandle; it is the major source of melting sand in West Virginia and the eastern United States.

By the 1830s numerous glass factories had sprung up along the Ohio River, with Wheeling as the hub, producing wine and drinking glasses, window glass, and other products demanded by the young and growing country. The glassware was shipped by barges plying the Ohio River and later by rail-

A spot of tea in Chester.

road. When wood for fuel became scarce in the early 1900s, the Oriskany sandstone again played a crucial role with its many deposits of inexpensive natural gas obtained from subsurface wells in the northern and western parts of the state.

WV 2 continues along the river, with views of 300-foot-high bluffs on both sides. After a few miles you reach the Mountaineer Race Track and Resort, which features live thoroughbred racing plus simulcast racing from other tracks nationwide. If the horses aren't running, numerous video slots and poker machines, golf, or tennis may hold your interest. Other amenities include several restaurants and a lodge.

Just past the resort turn left (east) on WV 208. This winding, two-lane road quickly leaves the hustle and bustle along the river as it climbs a narrow, wooded gully. After 3 miles, at the stop sign, turn right (south) on WV 3, passing through rolling country with alternating deciduous forests and cattle farms.

Soon you pass the entrance to Tomlinson Run State Park, where several short hiking trails lead past overhanging cliffs of sandstone and shale. Anglers try to catch trout, bass, and catfish in its thirty-three acres of ponds. The park also has a campground, cabins, a swimming pool, and a variety of other activities. The Rent-A-Camp program enables novice campers to rent a tent and other equipment for a small fee.

Turn right (west) on WV 8, which leads down through the Ohio River bluffs back to WV 2 at New Cumberland. Turn left (south) on WV 2. The drive continues to follow the river but climbs up the bluffs for a while for long-range views upstream and down.

At Weirton the drive passes through the Weirton Steel Corporation plant, which straddles both sides of the road. The town itself straddles the entire state (5 miles wide at this point) from Ohio to Pennsylvania. Weirton Steel is one of the few—and the largest—steel companies owned by the employees. After years of losing money, the plant workers bought out the owners in 1984. Since then, profitability has improved, but with a few lean years. Ask at the Chamber of Commerce if you are interested in a tour of the plant.

On the other side of Weirton, WV 2 joins four-lane US 22 for one exit, about three-quarters of a mile. Be sure to take the exit for WV 2.

The drive continues south on WV 2, following the bends in the Ohio River to the historic river town of Wellsburg, founded in 1791. At one time five glass companies were based in town; the Brooke Glass Company is the only one that still survives. This small, specialized firm produces fixtures for lamps and more than twenty different shades of colored glass.

In the late 1700s the Wellsburg Wharf was the loading area for flatboats heading south loaded with cargoes of glass and other freight. Only remnants of the wharf remain, including the foundations of two warehouses where goods were stored awaiting shipment. However, the Wellsburg historical district features numerous restored pre-colonial and federalist buildings.

BETHANY AND BETHANY COLLEGE

Just past Wellsburg, turn left (east) on WV 67. Once more you climb up a stream gully out of the Ohio River Valley to emerge amid rolling hills, woods, and well-kept farms. After about 5 miles cross WV 88 and continue about half a mile to the tree-covered streets of the village of Bethany, home of Bethany College. The entire town is on the National Register of Historic Places.

The college, established in 1840, is the oldest institution of higher learning in West Virginia. The centerpiece of the campus is the 400-foot-long Old Main Building. Its red brick Gothic architecture incorporates several archways and a clock tower more than 120 feet high. Construction of the building began before the Civil War; it was finally finished in 1911 and restored

Faculty gather on the steps of Bethany College.

and renovated in the 1980s. Ask at the Historic Bethany Information Center for tours of the college, including the Old Bethany Meeting House, built in 1850, and the Alexander Campbell Mansion, built in the 1790s. The latter building is named for and was the home of the college's founder.

When you leave Bethany, go back to the intersection of WV 67 and WV 88 and turn left (south) on WV 88, which follows a small open ridge. The picturesque village you see below and will pass through in a few minutes is West Liberty, home of West Liberty State College. The school was the oldest academy in West Virginia, established in 1837, and became a college a few years later.

About 5 miles past West Liberty is the Oglebay Resort and Conference Center. Run by the Wheeling Parks Commission, this 1,600-acre public park and complex attracts more than three million visitors a year, most—obviously—from out of state, and many from foreign countries. Its meticulously cared for grounds, buildings, and attractions have something for almost everyone.

OGLEBAY PARK AND RESORT

The park got its start in 1926 when industrialist Colonel Earl Oglebay bequeathed his summer estate, 750-acre Waddington Farm, now a museum, to Wheeling for public use. Today the park includes West Virginia's only accredited zoo, formal gardens, a lodge and conference center, nature center, numerous shops, a mansion, three golf courses, and a sports center. A large selection of West Virginia decorative glass is exhibited at the Carriage Glass House. Some attractions charge admission.

The Good Zoo, a donation of the Good family, is designed for children and specializes in natural North American habitats and endangered species. A petting zoo gives kids hands-on contact with friendly beasts, but adults are also welcome to view and pet the animals.

In 2000 the park opened the Schrader Environmental Education Nature Center, acclaimed for its butterfly exhibit, wildflowers, interpretive nature trails, and wildlife and environmental education programs for children.

Oglebay's busiest travel season occurs from November through February, when more than a half million lights blink and shine from trees, buildings, and specially built structures during Wheeling's Festival of Lights.

The drive ends a few miles later in Wheeling at the intersection of WV 88 and US 40. Turn right (west) on US 40 to go downtown. Despite its many attractions, most travelers see little of Wheeling as they zoom through town and the entire Northern Panhandle on I-70.

During the 1800s Wheeling, at the edge of the western frontier, was known as the Gateway to the West. The town flourished as the jumping-off spot and supply area for travelers seeking their destiny to the west or south along the Ohio River. Its stately Victorian mansions, now a part of Victorian Wheeling National Historic District, are a tribute to the wealth and expert craftsmanship of the era.

Travelers heading west left town via the graceful Wheeling Suspension Bridge, completed in 1849, more than forty years before New York's famed Brooklyn Bridge. The Wheeling Suspension Bridge was overhauled and renovated in 1999 and still carries traffic between downtown and historic Wheeling Island in the Ohio River. The original toll was 10 cents for a man and horse, $1.25 for a four-horse carriage; now it's free for both pedestrians and autos.

Wheeling is also a center for the arts, as exemplified by the Stifel Fine Arts Center and the Wheeling Artisan Center. Nor is music neglected: The granddaddy of country music stations, WWVA, still broadcasts its cowboy ballads and epics of romance and love to millions of listeners. The show that is the heart and soul of country music and WWVA, Jamboree USA, has featured old and new performers on Saturday nights since 1933. Tickets to the show, now held in the Modern Capitol Music Hall, can be obtained locally.

The Wheeling suspension bridge during renovations.

2

Moundsville to Fairmont

RUSTIC FARMLAND AND THE PALACE OF GOLD

GENERAL DESCRIPTION: A 57-mile drive through rustic woods, hills, farms, and small towns, seemingly untouched by the last seventy-five years, but with a few special attractions showing some of the many changes during the past 2,000 years.

SPECIAL ATTRACTIONS: Unspoiled farmlands and woods, the ancient Grave Creek Mound Historic Site, the modern Prabhupada's Palace of Gold, and the century-old Mannington Round Barn.

LOCATION: Northern West Virginia.

DRIVING route numbers and name: US 250; WV 7.

TRAVEL SEASON: All year.

CAMPING: None along the drive. Fairmont has a few private campgrounds.

SERVICES: Moundsville and Fairmont have complete services. Gasoline and restaurants can be found in most small towns along the drive.

NEARBY ATTRACTIONS: Louis Wetzel Wildlife Management Area, Pricketts Fort State Park, and Valley Falls State Park.

THE DRIVE

US 250 is a time machine that transports you back to the rural world of seventy-five years ago. Rustic dairy farms and old barns, hamlets and small bucolic towns, verdant rolling hills and pasture land, a gently winding, two-lane road, no fast food and no malls—is this the twenty-first century? US 250 from Moundsville to Fairmont may make you think you've returned to the 1930s (but on a paved, smooth, all-weather road).

But this time machine has a few time warps, old and new: You'll pass a 2,000-year-old burial mound, a castellated prison from the 1860s, a round dairy barn built in the early 1900s, and the modern spectacular domes and turrets of the Prabhupada Palace of Gold—all this surely is not from the 1930s! But it's all found along US 250.

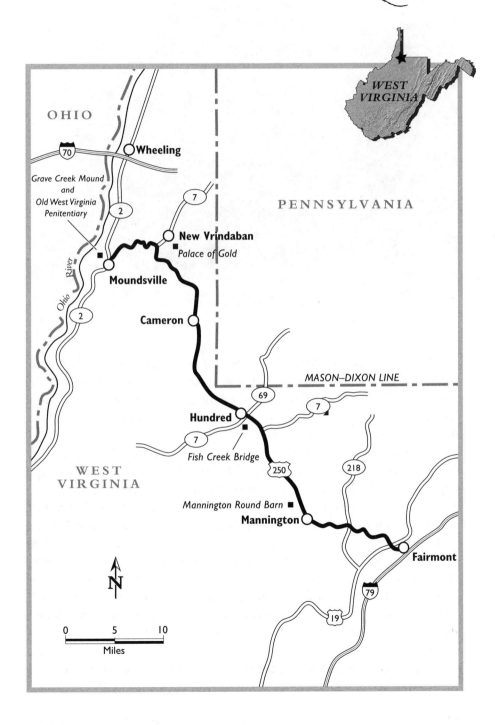

OHIO

70

Wheeling

*Grave Creek Mound
and
Old West Virginia
Penitentiary*

2

7

New Vrindaban

Palace of Gold

Moundsville

Ohio River

2

Cameron

PENNSYLVANIA

MASON–DIXON LINE

69

7

Hundred

7

Fish Creek Bridge

250

218

WEST
VIRGINIA

Mannington Round Barn

Mannington

Fairmont

79

19

N

0   5   10

Miles

WEST
VIRGINIA

This 1,200-year-old mound took the Adena Indians one hundred years to construct.

The drive begins in Moundsville on the Ohio River in the Northern Panhandle, then heads south and east over the rolling highlands of Mountaineer Country (named not for lofty peaks but for West Virginia University's beloved football team at Morgantown). It ends at Fairmont on the banks of the Monongahela River.

The drive has an urban but ancient beginning. In downtown Moundsville, follow the signs to Grave Creek Mound Historic Site, which occupies a large city block at 801 Jefferson Street between 8th and 10th Streets. This seven-acre park surrounds and protects a circular mound, 69 feet high and 300 feet in diameter. It is the largest of many similar mounds in the eastern United States.

Early European settlers realized that the mounds were man-made, but they could only speculate as to their age, purpose, and how they were constructed. Some thought they were the remnants of an ancient vanished race of Africans or Europeans; others believed they represented one of the Lost Tribes of Israel. The people who built these structures were called the Mound Builders by the Europeans.

Excavations in 1838 revealed the remains of two skeletons, plus shells, tools, and other material within the mound. In 1881 Congress appropriated

$5,000 for the Smithsonian Institution to investigate some 2,000 mounds and earthworks in the eastern United States. This was the birth of modern American archaeology. These studies showed that the Mound Builders were not a vanished race but ancestors of the American Indian.

Today the Mound Builders are known as the Adena people, and the mounds, painstakingly built by hand, are considered to be elaborate burial sites for their leaders. The Moundsville mound is believed to have been constructed in stages over a hundred-year period from 250 to 150 B.C. Dirt—60,000 tons—was carried to the mound in baskets. Originally the mound was surrounded by a 40-foot-wide, 5-foot-deep moat, now mostly filled in.

Visitors enter the park through the Delf Norona Museum adjacent to the mound. The museum houses a collection of Adena tools, pottery, and other artifacts. Colorful exhibits show how the mound was built and how the Adena people lived. The top of the tree-covered mound is a three-minute walk from the museum. There is a small admission charge.

Across the street from the state park is the Old West Virginia Penitentiary, a menacing gray stone turreted monolith, where the state's hardened felons were domiciled from 1865 to 1995. For a small fee you can tour the structure, visiting cells, the exercise yard, and "Old Sparky," the electric chair that was in use until 1965 when West Virginia eliminated capital punishment. The prison was declared uninhabitable by the state supreme court and closed down in 1995.

ON TO THE PALACE OF GOLD

By now you're probably eager to get out of town and on the road. Head east on US 250, which curves and winds as it climbs up and out of the Ohio River Valley onto the surrounding open rolling hills and dairy farms. After about 10 miles, just past the small town of Limestone, turn left on WV 7 at the well-marked sign for New Vrindaban and the Palace of Gold.

This narrow road twists and turns past trailers and farms as it meanders along the top of the steep hillsides for 3 miles. Then, with no warning, the brilliant golden turrets, crenulated domes, and gilded walls of the Palace of Gold spring into sight.

The Palace was built as a memorial to Srila Prabhupada, founder of the Krishna Consciousness (Hare Krishna) movement. Prabhupada began his movement in 1965 when he arrived penniless in New York. By 1973, when construction of the Palace of Gold began, he had some 50,000 converts throughout the world. One of 120 temples worldwide and the only one in the United States, it took six years to finish. His followers did the bulk of the

Approaching the entrance to the Palace of Gold.

work; most of them had no training in construction. About 200 Krishna believers live here today.

Tours of the Palace, for which a small fee is charged, lead you over gleaming floors of inlaid Italian marble and Iranian onyx, past stained glass windows adorned with blue peacocks, Lord Krishna's motif, each containing more than 1,500 pieces of hand-cut glass. Crystal chandeliers hang overhead, echoed by the mirrored ceilings and gold leaf surfaces. Shoe coverings are provided, but you will endear yourself to your tour guide if you remove your footgear and tread gently in stocking feet over the polished floors.

The 25-foot central dome features eighteen murals depicting the life of Lord Krishna. At the altar a lifelike statue of Prabhupada is seated on a bejeweled and golden throne serenely looking over his domain. The tour passes by Prabhupada's apartment, with its bathroom fixtures of solid gold and marble. Hundreds of meticulously handpainted flowers grace the bedroom ceiling.

Before or after the tour, you are welcome to wander at will through the grounds and gardens, including a prize-winning rose garden. If you get hungry, try the low-cost Palace Restaurant, one of West Virginia's few Indian vegetarian restaurants. Nearby are a conference center, interfaith temple, guest lodge, and gift shop.

When you leave New Vrindaban, follow WV 7 back to US 250 and turn left. The highway was laid out in the 1930s and follows the high ground over this hilly country. Before the days of interstate highways, it was a major northwest-southeast thoroughfare linking Wheeling with the Virginia border. The section covered by this drive now has light traffic, and its small towns and villages look virtually unchanged by the passing of sixty years.

Typical of the small towns along the way is Cameron, whose short main street runs side by side with the railroad and the creek, and where two old red-brick churches sit side by side in the center of the village.

CROSSING THE MASON-DIXON LINE

A few miles beyond Cameron, you leave Marshall County and enter Wetzel County. The east-west county line marks the Mason-Dixon Line, the traditional boundary between the South and North. Properly known as Mason and Dixon's Line, it was surveyed by English astronomers Charles Mason and Jeremiah Dixon from 1763 to 1767 to settle a boundary dispute between colonies. At latitude 39° 43' 19.11", it later came to symbolize the boundary between free and slave states. Today it marks much of the southern border of Pennsylvania with both Maryland and West Virginia

A few miles below the Mason-Dixon Line lies the little town of Hundred, named for Henry Church, a longtime resident. As a young man Church was a soldier in the British Army. During the Battle of Yorktown, Virginia, in 1781, he was captured by American troops. After the conflict he settled here; over the years he was recognized as the local patriarch. When his age extended beyond the century mark, he became known as "Old Hundred." After his death in 1869 at the age of 109, the settlement became known as Hundred.

As you leave Hundred, on the right you pass Rush Run Road, County Road 13, and the Fish Creek Covered Bridge. Constructed in 1881 and still in use, the Fish Creek bridge is a 36-foot-long kingpost truss span.

In the 1800s designers, craftsmen, and builders considered their covered bridges, which were vital to transportation, to be both functional and beautiful. The delicate wooden support arches and trusses were well protected by the walls and roof. With the coming of the railroads and their easily constructed and more durable steel bridges, wooden covered bridges became less important. Many fell into disrepair. By the 1930s about a hundred covered bridges were still standing in West Virginia, but only seventeen survive today. The ones that remain are again highly valued, but more for their beauty, workmanship, heritage, and history than as aids to transportation.

Covered bridges are not the only remnants of the early 1900s. Look for several old barns with faded painted sides that urge you to chew Mail Pouch Tobacco. During the hard times of the Great Depression, farmers with barns visible from the road were happy to receive a free barn painting from tobacco companies. It made little difference if the side facing the highway was an advertisement.

The drive follows several small streams and crosses Buffalo Creek in Mannington. The town grew rapidly after petroleum was discovered here in 1869. The original well was one of the first drilled on geological evidence; its location was based on the then-new "anticlinal theory," the discovery that oil was found under folded arches—anticlines—and domes of subsurface rock. Later, coal mining provided jobs for many workers. With the decline in both oil production and coal, unemployment has become a major problem for this area, as well as others in the state.

In downtown Mannington the West Augusta Historical Society maintains a small museum of historical artifacts in an old school house. Children may enjoy a brief stop to look at an early 1900s caboose and an 1870 log cabin on the grounds.

THE MANNINGTON ROUND BARN

A few blocks past the museum, turn right on Flaggy Meadow Road and follow the signs to the Mannington Round Barn, also maintained by the West Augusta Historical Society. Built in 1912, this is the only round barn in the state and is listed on the National Register of Historical Places.

This dairy barn was built by farmer Amos C. Hamilton. Farmers liked round barns because the large loft on the top floor gave them lots of storage space for hay. In addition to hay this three-story barn housed cows on the ground floor and the Hamilton family on the second. Today it is filled with Hamilton mementos and old farm equipment such as butter churns, a horse-drawn potato picker, and a child's sled. You'll also see the Hamiltons' living quarters and the spring-fed automatic watering system for cows. Several flights of narrow stairs lead up to the cupola for an interesting view of the neighborhood.

A nominal donation is requested for both the museum and the round barn. Both buildings are open on Sunday afternoons, or any time by appointment. See the Appendix for the phone number and address.

The Mannington Round Barn displays farming implements of a hundred years ago.

From Mannington it is about 12 miles on US 250 through several small towns to Fairmont and the end of the drive. Be sure to drive by High Gate, a coal baron's Tudor Revival mansion on Fairmont Avenue between 8th and 9th Streets. The town is home to Fairmont State College, established in 1867 and now West Virginia's largest four-year public college. Preserved on campus is the Snodgrass School, a 23-by-26-foot one-room schoolhouse, originally built in 1871.

In nearby Barrackville is the 146-foot-long Barrackville Covered Bridge—almost three times as long as the Fish Creek Covered Bridge. North of town is Pricketts Fort State Park, restored to look as it did in 1774, where costumed interpreters demonstrate what life was like in frontier colonial days. South of town lies Valley Falls State Park, where the Tygart River flows through a narrow canyon. Hiking, picnicking, and mountain biking are popular at this day-use facility

Along the Ohio River

NEW MARTINSVILLE TO PARKERSBURG

GENERAL DESCRIPTION: A 50-mile drive on a paved, two-lane highway along the Ohio River past scenic islands and historical oil and gas boomtowns. The area is mostly rural but with some industrial development.

SPECIAL ATTRACTIONS: The bends and bluffs of the Ohio River, Hannibal Dam and locks, Ohio River Islands National Wildlife Refuge, historic Sistersville and its antique operating oil well, and Parkersburg and Blennerhassett Island Historical State Park.

LOCATION: Western West Virginia, along the Ohio River.

DRIVING ROUTE NUMBERS AND NAME: WV 2, 31.

TRAVEL SEASON: All year. Some attractions are closed during the colder months.

CAMPING: The closest public campground is at North Bend State Park, about 20 miles east of Parkersburg on US 50, with seventy-seven sites and all facilities. Two private campgrounds are near Parkersburg.

SERVICES: All services are available in most towns.

NEARBY ATTRACTIONS: Wayne National Forest (in Ohio, across the river), Blennerhassett Island Historic State Park, and North Bend Rail Trail.

THE DRIVE

For about 250 miles the Ohio River is shared by West Virginia and Ohio and marks the western border of West Virginia. Drive 1, Northern Panhandle, describes scenes along the panhandle and northern section of the Ohio River from Chester, at the northern tip of West Virginia, to Wheeling.

This drive begins on the Ohio River at New Martinsville, 45 miles south of Wheeling, and follows WV 2 and the river 50 miles south to Parkersburg. Wayne National Forest borders the river on the Ohio side for much of the drive, and approximately ten islands in the river are a part of the Ohio River Islands National Wildlife Refuge, so much of this stretch is thinly settled and relatively undeveloped.

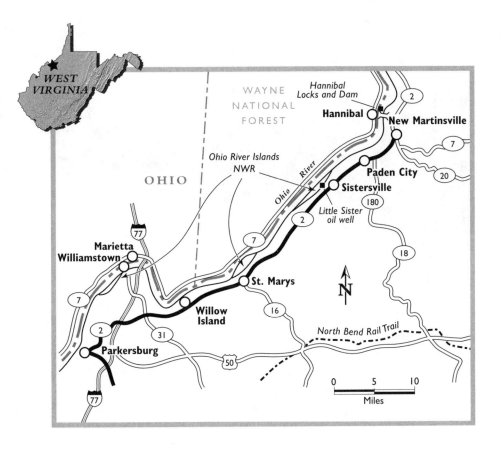

At New Martinsville the river flows along a mile-wide flat valley with rocky bluffs 150 feet high on the West Virginia side. The town was settled in the late 1700s and was then known as Martin's Fort after Presley Martin, leader of the fort and small community. As the new country of the United States of America grew and prospered in the early 1800s, the Ohio River became an important highway for trade and travel between Fort Pitt (Pittsburgh) and New Orleans, and Martin's Fort flourished as an important port of call along the river.

River travel is important today, but instead of side-wheelers and wooden flatboats hauling lumber, huge barges and iron freighters carry coal and goods of all kinds to cities and ports around the world. This trade has been made possible by construction of fifty-three dams and sets of locks along the 981

The Hannibal Locks in Ohio. New Martinsville lies on the other side of the bridge.

river-miles of the Ohio River from the confluence in Pittsburgh of the Monongahela and Allegheny Rivers to Cairo, Illinois, where the Ohio joins the Mississippi. The dams, built and operated by the U.S. Army Corps of Engineers, provide pools of water behind them deep enough for year-round navigation, and the locks raise or lower the boats to account for the 460-foot difference in elevation between Pittsburgh and Cairo.

Dominating the river in New Martinsville is one of those dams, the 1,089-foot-long Hannibal Locks and Dam. An observation platform and visitor center is on the Ohio side of the river. So perhaps the best way to start a drive down the Ohio River is to cross the river itself. From WV 2 at the northern end of New Martinsville, cross over the river on the high arch of the Korean War Veteran's Memorial Bridge. Drive slowly and take in the excellent views of the dam, river, town, and surrounding countryside. The parking area for the dam is to the right as you leave the bridge in Hannibal, Ohio.

The observation platform lets you look down on the locks, which raise or lower vessels 21 feet. The main lock, 1,200 feet long, can accommodate the longest coal barge on the river. The structure averages 350 lockages a month—more than eleven per day—so your chances of seeing a vessel pass through a lock are good.

Exhibits on the grounds of the visitor center include the remains of a historic wicket dam and a maneuver boat, used for driving pilings in the river.

Other exhibits depict the history of navigation on the Ohio River and have information about the U. S. Army Corps of Engineers.

Drive back over the bridge and turn right (south) on WV 2 through New Martinsville. The town is a center for river-based recreation, with a county-maintained fishing pier and marina. Each summer the town hosts the three-day River Heritage Days Festival and Regatta; the high point is power boat racing on the Ohio River, which attracts some of the country's fastest hydro-boats. The historical area features several 1890s Victorian buildings, the most notable of which is the multiturreted Wetzel County Courthouse.

Glass making is a major industry along the Ohio River Valley, and several local factories used to offer tours of their operations. Alas, the plants in New Martinsville and Paden City (the next town on the drive) have either closed or discontinued public tours. But do not despair: Fenton Art Glass in Williamstown, outside Parkersburg and near the end of this drive, provides a comprehensive tour of its museum and factory. Details are provided later in this chapter.

As you travel south on WV 2 from New Martinsville, the drive and the Ohio River follow a valley several miles wide, often bordered by bluffs and cliffs 200 to 300 feet high. Side streams enter the valley through broad and steep gullies.

There's a good chance that the marbles you or your children play with (or store in decorative glass jars) were made by the Marble King in Paden City, 9 miles from New Martinsville. This appropriately named company is one of the world's largest marble makers, turning the waste glass from other glass companies into millions of these tiny spheres each year.

OHIO RIVER ISLANDS NATIONAL WILDLIFE REFUGE

South of Paden City, you may notice several islands in the Ohio River. Teenage surveyor George Washington noticed them too, and wrote about "The Ohio River Crowded with Islands." Today nineteen of these islands scattered along 362 miles of the river from Pennsylvania to Kentucky are part of the Ohio River Islands National Wildlife Refuge. Their natural beauty is enhanced by the Wayne National Forest, which borders the Ohio side of the river from just north of Paden City to a few miles north of Parkersburg.

Eleven of the refuge islands are clustered in a 20-mile stretch of river between New Martinsville and St. Marys along this drive. Most of them are accessible only by boat, but at St. Marys a short bridge gives you the oppor-tunity to visit Middle Island.

A few miles past Paden City you come to the quiet little town of Sistersville. In the 1880s as in many villages along the Ohio, the 500 residents were primarily engaged in farming and agriculture or servicing the steamboat and river trade.

This era ended virtually overnight in 1889 when oil was discovered in the area. Thirty years earlier oil and gas had propelled Parkersburg into boom town status, and the possibility of the same thing happening in Sistersville ignited the hopes and dreams of many. Geologists, speculators, bankers, businessmen, fortune seekers, and camp followers poured into the area, eager to get their share of the wealth from black gold. Soon oil derricks covered the hills and streets and many backyards, and the clanking of pumps and the smell of crude oil were always in the background.

As the oil began to flow, money flowed along with it, as more than a hundred oil companies located here, and the population grew to some 15,000. The new wealth brought a flurry of construction with it, resulting in ornate Victorian mansions and buildings for the many corporations. The now-affluent community built modern public schools, a city-operated hospital, a municipal electric power station, and a trolley line to surrounding towns. The boom also brought breweries, saloons, brothels, gambling casinos, hotels, and theaters, including an opera house that imported first-run shows and vaudeville acts from New York.

By 1915 the oil was played out and the boom collapsed. Most people lost their jobs or abandoned their businesses and left—some penniless, some with fortunes. Within a few years the wells and derricks had disappeared. The townspeople who remained had mostly prospered from the boom, with many fashionable homes and buildings still remaining.

Today the town, with its well-maintained and reconstructed century-old buildings, is listed as a National Historic District. You can obtain a free map and guide of the historical district at the distinctive diamond-shaped City Hall, which straddles the intersection of Main and Diamond. This historical structure was built in 1897 in the American Colonial style. Nearby is the Wells Inn, restored to its 1895 grandeur and modernized for the twenty-first century.

STILL PUMPING: THE LITTLE SISTER OIL WELL

Along the waterfront is the restored Little Sister oil well and derrick, one of the last remnants of the hundreds of wells that formerly covered the landscape. No mere decoration, this well is operational. Each September it pumps

The Little Sister oil well in Sisterville still pumps oil during the annual Oil and Gas Festival.

up some souvenir black gold during the West Virginia Oil and Gas Festival.

Adjacent to the well is the terminal for the Sistersville Ferry, where ferries have plied across the Ohio River since 1808. The current ferry, operated by the town of Sistersville, is the last commercial ferry in West Virginia, and has a capacity of four cars. For a 50-cent fee, pedestrians can take a fifteen minute round trip cruise to Fly, Ohio, with panoramic views of the Little Sister well and the town of Sistersville. The ferry operates on an as-needed schedule, so look around for the ferry operator.

Back on the drive, continue south on WV 2, passing several Victorian mansions as you leave town. The river widens, and the countryside becomes more open and spacious with lower, gentler hills. Several working oil and gas wells show that the petroleum industry is still important to the economy, but there is little new drilling.

As you approach St. Marys you'll notice more islands in the river; most are part of the Ohio River Islands National Wildlife Refuge. Near the end of the Pleistocene epoch, as the continental glaciers to the north melted, large volumes of melt water flowed down the Ohio River, carrying enormous amounts of gravel, sand, silt, and other debris along with it. After the ice melted the flow decreased, and much of the debris was deposited in the river to form the numerous islands.

A short bridge by the river connects St. Marys with Middle Island, one of the most accessible and beautiful islands in the refuge. Turn right on George Street to reach the bridge.

The refuge and islands protect some of the last remnants of habitat along the river for shorebirds, waterfowl, songbirds, and freshwater fish and mussels. More than 160 species of birds are found in the refuge, including several great blue heron rookeries. The shallow back channels are important nursery and feeding areas for some of the fifty species of warmwater fish. Beaver, mink, muskrat, cottontail rabbit, opossum, raccoon, and white-tailed deer are common island mammals.

Hundreds of years before Europeans came to the area, the islands were well known to the Indians, with archeological remains found on several islands. When George Washington surveyed the river, fifty-seven islands graced the river; forty-one remain today, with the rest carried away on barges for their gravel and sand. Because the west bank of the river (the Ohio side) marks the boundary between Ohio and West Virginia, most of the river, including the islands, lies within West Virginia.

From St. Marys continue south on WV 2. The drive soon becomes more urban, with several manufacturing plants and other businesses. As you

Parkersburg's Oil and Gas Museum is a graveyard for ancient oil well equipment.

approach the town of Willow Island, you'll see the huge cooling towers with their plumes of steam issuing from the Willow Run Nuclear Plant

In Waverly WV 2 leaves the river and continues straight about 5 miles to Parkersburg and the end of the drive. As an alternate finish bear west (right) on WV 31 about 3 miles to Williamstown, to the showrooms and home of Fenton Art Glass, one of the oldest and largest glass manufacturers in the state. A free extensive tour takes you through the factory past craftsmen and artists and the glowing orange furnaces where their famed art pieces are produced.

Parkersburg, where the Little Kanawha River flows into the Ohio, became a boomtown in 1859 as the first producer of oil and gas in the United States. The Oil and Gas Museum describes this fascinating story and also contains extensive exhibits of drilling equipment and paraphernalia, with the larger pieces, such as a 1905 steam engine, stored outside. A panoramic geologic map shows the location of more than 10,000 wells drilled in the state since 1859. Also in town is the Cultural Center of Fine Arts, known for its Winslow Homer collection as well as local artwork. Nominal fees are charged.

Nearby in the Ohio River is the Blennerhassett Island Historical State Park, with its keystone exhibit of the restored and reconstructed 7,000-square-foot Blennerhassett Mansion, originally built in 1801. The island is accessible only by a twenty-minute sternwheeler voyage from downtown Parkersburg during the warmer months. Visitors can enjoy the natural beauty of the island and tour the ornate mansion where Harman Blennerhassett plotted with Aaron Burr to establish a new country in the southwest.

4

Kingwood to cathedral state park

THROUGH THE CHEAT RIVER GORGE

GENERAL DESCRIPTION: This 26-mile drive follows the gorge of the Cheat River and then visits the virgin hemlocks and hardwoods of Cathedral State Park.

SPECIAL ATTRACTIONS: Cheat River gorge and Cathedral State Park.

LOCATION: Northwest West Virginia.

DRIVING ROUTE NUMBERS AND NAME: US 50; VA 7, 72.

TRAVEL SEASON: All year. For an unforgettable experience visit Cathedral State Park during peak fall colors or after a winter snowstorm.

CAMPING: None along the drive. At Albright north of Kingwood is a small private campground.

SERVICES: All services are available along the drive.

NEARBY ATTRACTIONS: Arthurdale Historic District, Fairfax Stone, Monongahela National Forest, and Our Lady of the Pines shrine in Silver Lake.

THE DRIVE

From Kingwood this 26-mile drive follows the gorge of the Cheat River, ascends out of the gorge, and ends at majestic virgin forest at Cathedral State Park. The entire drive is over hard-surfaced all-weather roads and can be completed in a few hours.

On a high bluff above the Cheat River sits Kingwood, a former mining town now known better as the jumping-off spot for raft trips down this raging torrent. Coal mines still operate, but at a fraction of the tonnage during their peak years, and the town's economy is as much tied to the nearby U.S. Army air base as to coal.

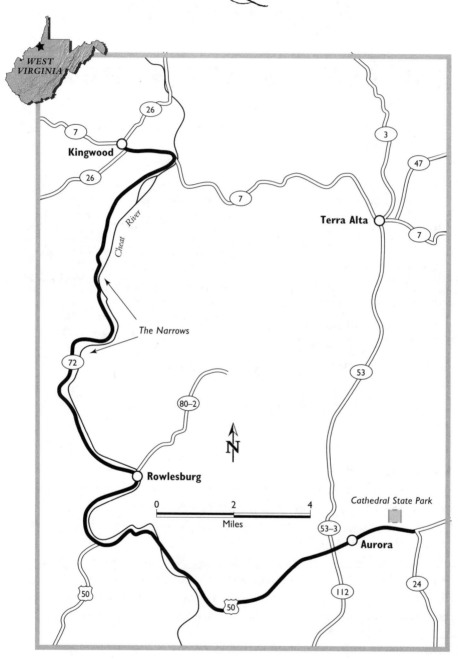

WEST VIRGINIA

Kingwood

Terra Alta

The Narrows

Cheat River

Rowlesburg

Cathedral State Park

Aurora

0   2   4

Miles

N

The railroads have suffered, too. Kingwood and the state lost a treasured icon when the West Virginia Northern Railroad made its last run in November 1999, ironically a few months after the railroad celebrated its one hundredth birthday.

The WVN began in 1899 as a narrow gauge line hauling coal from local mines. At the height of coal mining activity during World War II, the WVN was loading coal from nineteen mines along its 11-mile route from Kingwood to Tunnelton. On most days a fifty-car train plied the route; on peak days the total could reach 200. At Tunnelton the coal cars were switched to the main line of the Baltimore and Ohio Railroad.

As some mines closed and others switched to hauling coal by truck, the WVN was forced to cease activity in 1991. A local corporation was chartered to operate the line as a passenger excursion train until late 1999 when it, too, was forced to close for financial reasons. The corporation applied for an abandonment exemption in 2001, with plans to sell track and equipment to meet debts. Unless the state takes over the operation, this is the end of the line for another of West Virginia's small railroads.

THROUGH THE CHEAT RIVER VALLEY

From Kingwood go south on WV 72, which follows the Cheat River. Across the river you'll see the runways of Camp Dawson, a U.S. Army air-field and training center. Soon the river valley closes in, and steep hills rise from either bank.

The Cheat River, along with the New and Gauley, make up the "Big Three" of West Virginia's white-water rafting rivers. This section of the Cheat, known as the Narrows, borders WV 72 for several miles and is one of the few places where motorists can drive for any distance along a major white-water river. Considered suitable for beginning rafters and families, the rapids in the Narrows are rated from II to IV. (I is the mildest; VI is the roughest.)

The Cheat can be run year-round but is most popular in late spring when snow melt from mountains to the south brings the highest water levels. The wildest section of the Cheat, the Canyon, begins north of Kingwood and runs through remote roadless country to the dammed-up Cheat Lake near Morgantown. For experts only, the Canyon has miles of non-stop rapids that are rated from III to V, or even VI when the water is highest.

Depending on the weather and water level, you may or may not see rafters. You will see a few coal mines and a cement plant across the river on the steep slopes, as well as the town of Rowlesburg spread out along the narrow valley.

Low water on the Cheat River Narrows.

At the stop sign and intersection with US 50, turn east (left). US 50, also known as the Wilderness Road or Northwestern Turnpike, was surveyed in the early 1800s by the French engineer Claude Crozet. Following game trails and Indian paths, he laid out a route from the Shenandoah Valley of Virginia to the Ohio River. Before the days of interstates, US 50 was a main east-west highway, a ribbon of road across the continent from the Atlantic shores of Maryland to the California coast. (It now ends at Sacramento.) The highway has a following and mystique second only to that of old US 66.

US 50 follows the gorge of the Cheat River, here reduced to minor rapids, for a few miles and then begins a long climb out of the deep valley onto rolling plateau and gentle hills. Outside Aurora you will begin to see something awesome on the left side of the road: a thick forest of huge majestic trees. This is Cathedral State Park, 133 acres of the last stand of virgin mixed timber in the state.

A 500-YEAR-OLD HEMLOCK

Most impressive are the huge hemlocks, many hundreds of years old. The Centennial, the largest hemlock east of the Mississippi, measures 68 feet in

One of the numerous small streams in Cathedral State Park.

circumference and rises 120 feet from the ground, with a spread of almost 70 feet. More than 500 years old, it was a sapling only a few years after Columbus landed in the New World.

Other trees—red oak, maple, beech, black cherry, and yellow birch—accompany the hemlocks, like the supporting instruments to a master virtuoso. Several miles of trails lead through the woods, shaded on even the sunniest of days by the green needles of the hemlocks far overhead.

At one time much of West Virginia looked like this. Because it was part of an inn and resort, these woods were saved from the lumberman's ax when the state was virtually clear-cut. Later the property was deeded to the state. The park is open 365 days a year. Autumn colors are brilliant; winter snows are breathtaking. Tours are held on Wednesdays during the warmer months. It almost goes without saying that the park is on the National Registry for Natural History Landmarks.

The drive ends here. Five miles south of the park via WV 24 in Silver Lake is Our Lady of the Pines chapel. Measuring just 24 by 12 feet, with room inside to squeeze in twelve worshippers, it is said to be the smallest church in the country.

5

Romney~Keyser Loop

ROUTE OF THE POTOMAC EAGLE

GENERAL DESCRIPTION: A 55-mile loop drive from Romney, home of the Potomac Eagle Scenic Railroad, to Keyser, through low hills and farmland and along the South Branch of the Potomac River.

SPECIAL ATTRACTIONS: Potomac Eagle Scenic Railroad, Fort Ashby, and views of the South Branch of the Potomac.

LOCATION: Northeastern West Virginia.

DRIVING ROUTE NUMBERS AND NAME: US 50, 220; WV 28, 46.

TRAVEL SEASON: All year. The Potomac Eagle runs during warmer months only. Fall foliage trips may require advance reservations.

CAMPING: Near Romney are several private campgrounds.

SERVICES: All services are available along the drive.

NEARBY ATTRACTIONS: Nancy Hanks Memorial and Waffle Rock at Jennings Randolph Lake.

THE DRIVE

This 55-mile drive begins at Romney, heads west on US 50 and then north on US 220 to Keyser, then loops back via WV 46 and WV 28 past restored Fort Ashby and along the South Branch of the Potomac River back to Romney. Most of the drive is through farm and pasture land, with some forested areas. It also passes through small gaps in the low-lying mountains. The complete drive can be made in about two hours.

As an alternative to the complete loop drive, you can take the most scenic portion of the drive, which is north of Romney on WV 28 along the South Branch Valley. For many people the primary focus of their visit is the Potomac Eagle Scenic Railroad, which offers a variety of trips. If you are waiting for a train ride but have limited time, the drive along the South Branch Valley may suit your purposes.

5 ROMNEY~KEYSER LOOP

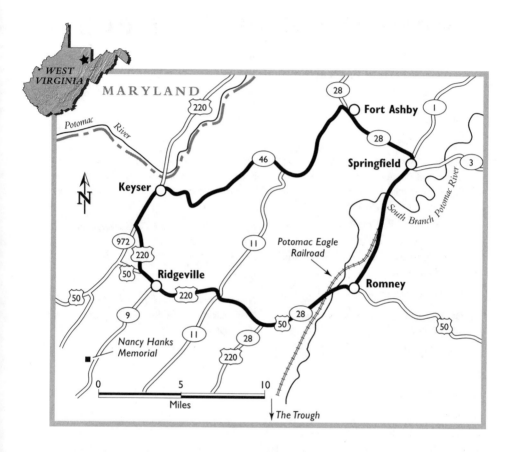

US 50 started as an Indian trail, and Romney, one of the oldest towns in the state, was incorporated in 1762. The town saw lots of action during the Civil War as it seesawed from one side to the other more than fifty times.

If you want to see eagles, take the train—the Potomac Eagle Scenic Railroad on the outskirts of Romney. This excursion train offers a three-hour trip along the South Branch of the Potomac. The highlight of the tour is The Trough, a narrow, steep-walled, 17-mile-long gorge that is one of the few nesting places in the state for the American bald eagle. There is no guarantee, but eagles are spotted on nine out of ten train trips. You'll see these majestic birds soaring through the gorge on thermals, and you may be lucky enough to see one of them swoop down to the river and snag a tasty fish. You can't drive through The Trough; the only way to get there is by train or canoe.

In addition to eagles you'll see grazing cattle, hawks, and maybe deer and beaver. Look for fish in the clear waters below as the train crosses the river on trestles. You can ride in an enclosed coach, but photographers may prefer the open gondola car. For the ultimate in comfort and an additional charge, choose the Club Car.

The train runs several times a day during the warmer months. Reservations are recommended in October when the fall foliage bathes the gorge in yellow and orange. Special excursion trips are featured throughout the year.

The automobile part of this scenic drive starts in Romney and goes west on US 50. As you cross the South Branch of the Potomac, you also cross the tracks of the Potomac Eagle and then leave the Potomac River Valley through a small gap.

At the town of Junction, bear right on US 50/220. The hills become somewhat larger as you proceed west. At Ridgeville at the foot of Knobly Mountain, a side trip on WV 8 leads south (left) to the birthplace of Nancy Hanks, mother of President Abraham Lincoln.

After the gap through Knobly Mountain, go north (right) on US 220 where it splits from US 50. Ahead you'll see the long ridge of Fore Knobs,

The Potomac Eagle passes the cliffs at the entrance to The Trough.
Photo: Stephen J. Shalnta Jr., courtesy West Virginia Division of Tourism.

Romney-Keyser Loop

Fort Ashby, one of the sixty-nine forts built during the French and Indian Wars.

which forms the imposing Allegheny Front to the southwest.

This takes you into Keyser, the county seat of Mineral County. The campus of Potomac State College, a center for the performing arts, adorns the hillside on the left. On the other side of town, turn east (right) on WV 46. This less-traveled road passes farms and woods to Fort Ashby.

The palisaded wooden logs of Fort Ashby look much as they did in 1755, one of sixty-nine forts ordered built by young army officer George Washington to protect this area during the French and Indian Wars. To arrange a tour of the fort, call in advance (see Appendix).

Turn right on WV 28 in Fort Ashby. Past Springfield the drive parallels the South Fork of the Potomac, a winding, lazy river at this point, and a popular recreation area for fishing, boating, and swimming. The drive follows the river past the station for the Potomac Eagle to Romney and the end of the drive.

6

Berkeley springs to Paw Paw

SPRINGS, SPAS, AND TUNNELS

GENERAL DESCRIPTION: A 30-mile drive from the baths of Berkeley Springs past the Panorama Overlook along Cacapon Creek to the Paw Paw Tunnel at the Chesapeake and Ohio National Historic Canal.

SPECIAL ATTRACTIONS: The spas, baths, shops, and sights of Berkeley Springs; Panorama Overlook; Cacapon Mountain and Cacapon Creek; and the Paw Paw Tunnel of the Chesapeake and Ohio Canal at the Potomac River.

LOCATION: Eastern West Virginia.

DRIVING ROUTE NUMBERS AND NAME: WV 9; MD 51.

TRAVEL SEASON: All year.

CAMPING: A few primitive campsites are at the end of the drive at the C & O Canal at Paw Paw.

SERVICES: All services are available in Berkeley Springs at the start of the drive, but little is available along the route.

NEARBY ATTRACTIONS: Cacapon Resort State Park, Martinsburg (see Drive 7).

THE DRIVE:

If there is a theme for this 30-mile drive, it is "water." Start with some ablutions at the bubbling town of Berkeley Springs, famed since colonial days for its warm mineralized spas and baths. Then head west across Cacapon Ridge with its outstanding views of the Potomac River. Follow sinuous Cacapon Creek through thick woods to the town of Paw Paw. The drive ends at the Potomac River at the Chesapeake and Ohio Canal National Historic Park, where you can hike through woods along the canal towpath and through the 3,000-foot-long Paw Paw Tunnel. This relatively short drive can be combined with Drive 7, which travels from Harpers Ferry to Berkeley Springs.

The first bathers at Berkeley Springs were members of various Indian tribes who refreshed themselves in this valley where the warm water gurgled out of the limestone rock. Teenaged George Washington first visited the

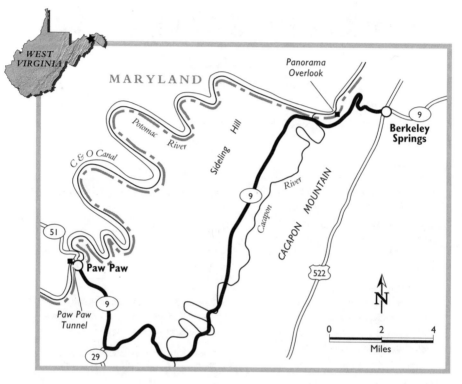

springs on a surveying trip in 1748; over the next fifty years he frequently brought his family here where they enjoyed bathing in and drinking the lightly mineralized water.

In 1776 Washington bought two lots and named the town Bath, still the official name for the town, after the ancient spa of the same name in England. Other members of the Washington family also owned land in the area. After he became president, Washington spent several weeks each summer here, establishing what some have called the "first Summer White House."

GEORGE WASHINGTON'S BATHTUB

Today Berkeley Springs State Park lies in the center of the town square where the ground gurgles and bubbles from the rising waters. Visitors can fill their jugs at the public tap. In warm weather children wade in the numerous pools. Prominent on the grounds is George Washington's Bathtub, where the teenaged surveyor reputedly washed away the grime and tiredness after a hard day's work.

A quiet springfed pool by the bathhouse at Berkeley Springs.

The square is flanked by two public bathhouses. The Roman Bath House, built in 1815, features nine private bathing rooms, each with a tub large enough for four (but cozy enough for two). The tubs are available for half-hour or hour rentals. Upstairs is a small museum.

Across the square is the Main Bath House, where you can combine a soaking with a steam bath or massage. Water emerges from the ground at the rate of 2,000 gallons per minute at a temperature of 74 degrees, perhaps warm enough for George, but a tad cool for a relaxing soak. It's heated today to a therapeutic and soothing 104 degrees.

Prices at the state bathhouses are reasonable, less than $40.00 for a one-hour combination massage and soak and half that for a simple bath and shower. Advance reservations are recommended, particularly on weekends and holidays. If the public baths can't accommodate you, there are numerous private spas and bathhouses in town. Many are more luxurious and opulent than the state facilities and offer additional amenities, including mud wraps, manicures, traditional massages, and a variety of exotic massages such as the Thai technique. The local phone book lists more massage therapists than lawyers, which some residents consider a mixed blessing.

When you've had enough water, you can visit some of the numerous art galleries, crafts and specialty shops, antique stores, and small restaurants. Only three hours' drive from Washington, D. C., the area is attracting many weekend visitors who, like the first president, come here to relax and escape from the big city.

Begin the drive by heading west from the center of town on WV 9. As the drive ascends Warm Springs Ridge, a spur of Cacapon Mountain, you pass the Berkeley Castle, which overlooks the town like a sentinel. This replica of an English Norman castle was built in 1885 as a wedding gift. After decades of neglect it was almost destroyed in 1959 but was saved at the last minute and extensively refurbished.

The rock beneath Warm Spring Ridge is the Oriskany sandstone. This rock is an ancient beach deposit of pure quartz sand—silica—that was laid down at the edge of the ancestral North American continent during the Devonian period. Because of its purity, the Oriskany sandstone is in demand for glass making, stoneware, and other operations that require high-grade silica. About forty quarries in the state extract less pure sandstone to use as a construction aggregate, but the only major glass sand company in West Virginia lies about 5 miles south of the drive along Warm Spring Ridge. These quarries opened during the Civil War and now produce about 1.5 million tons of high-grade silica each year.

In a high valley past Warm Spring Ridge lies the entrance to the Coolfont Resort, site of another notable water-based activity in the area: the annual

Maryland lies to the right in this view of the Potomac River from the Panorama Overlook.

Berkeley Springs International Water Tasting. At this competitive event judges sip samples of tap water, identified only by a number, that have been submitted by municipalities around the world. The water is graded for flavor, odor ("none" is best), how it feels in the mouth, and aftertaste. Winners are sometimes surprising, often not usually associated with high-grade tap water. In recent years they have included Atlantic City, New Jersey (twice), and Beverly Hills, California. Held the last weekend in February, this is the finale of the wintertime Festival of Water.

THE PANORAMA OVERLOOK

About 3 miles from Berkeley Springs, the drive reaches the Panorama Overlook below Prospect Peak, the northern end of the long ridge of Cacapon Mountain. The view here, about 1,000 feet above the valley, encompasses the states of West Virginia, Maryland, and Pennsylvania; Sideling Hill; and two rivers, the Cacapon and the Potomac.

A roadside marker proclaims that "the National Geographic Society rates this scene as one of America's outstanding beauty spots"—perhaps an exaggeration, perhaps not. If you're hungry, a restaurant across the road from the overlook gives diners a chance to admire the view. High over the restaurant you'll see the Fluted Rocks, bare vertical outcrops of the Tuscarora sandstone that forms Prospect Peak.

This has been a favorite spot since colonial days, when an afternoon's horseback ride from Berkeley Springs was often followed by an evening of soaking and parties in the hot springs. Stories say that George Washington's nephew, Laurence Augustine, rode out here in 1796 to enjoy the view. His delight at the sight of mountains and rivers was quickly surpassed by his delight at the sight of fifteen-year-old Polly Wood, who was with another group. The chance meeting here led to their marriage a year later.

The road winds down the mountain to the village of Great Cacapon along the banks of the Potomac River at the confluence of the Cacapon River. Continuing west and south on WV 9, the towns grow smaller and the hills grow larger as the drive follows the Cacapon River Valley upstream along the long ridge of Cacapon Mountain. The drive is lined with thick hardwoods and pines and crosses sinuous Cacapon River several times.

At the intersection with WV 29, bear right (northwest), following WV 9 to the town of Paw Paw on the Potomac River. This was an important staging area during the Civil War for Union troops, when as many as 16,000 federal soldiers camped in the vicinity. The town (and tunnel, which you will reach in a few minutes) are named after the paw paw tree, *Asimina triloba*,

Now used by hikers and bikers, the Paw Paw Tunnel was once a vital link on the Chesapeake and Ohio Canal.

which grows in abundance in the area. The paw paw tree was once widely prized for its large, sweet fruit but is rarely harvested today.

THE CHESAPEAKE AND OHIO CANAL NATIONAL HISTORIC PARK

Follow WV 9 through town across the Potomac River into Maryland, where the route number changes to MD 51. The drive ends about one-quarter of a mile farther at the picnic and camping area of the Chesapeake and Ohio Canal National Historic Park along the banks of the Potomac River.

The C&O Canal follows the Maryland shore of the Potomac River for 184 miles from Georgetown in Washington, D. C., to Cumberland, Maryland. It was built with picks and shovels over a twenty-two-year period beginning in 1828. The finished canal was 6 feet deep and about 50 feet wide and included seventy-four locks and the Paw Paw tunnel. This section, from Hancock to Cumberland, was the last to be opened; the parking area is at mile 156.2. The canal was a vital link for communities along its banks, transporting coal, lumber, and other goods to the port of Georgetown, where they were loaded on seagoing vessels.

But the canal soon found itself competing with the new east-west route of the Baltimore and Ohio Railroad. The end came in 1924 when extensive flood damage and massive loss of business to the B&O forced the canal to close. Today the park is preserved as the Chesapeake and Ohio Canal National Historic Park. Now mostly dry, the canal and adjacent Potomac River provide an unbroken historic shoestring park for hiking, biking, fishing, and sightseeing.

From the parking area it is a level walk of 0.6 mile along the remnants of the canal to the tunnel entrance. The tunnel bisects Sorrel Ridge, cutting out 6 miles of bends in the Potomac. As you stand in the tunnel portal on the dry towpath, you can see a little dot of light at the far exit, 3,118 feet away. The tunnel is 24 feet high and contains some six million bricks. You can walk through the tunnel without lights (watch that little bright dot at the end slowly grow larger), but most people prefer to bring a flashlight. The air in the tunnel feels cool in warm weather and warm during the colder months. Occasional drops of water from the roof will feel cold at any time. Singing in the tunnel is recommended; the acoustics improve most voices.

Ranger-guided tours of the tunnel are held on Saturdays and Sundays during the warmer months. Check with the Park Service for the schedule. In addition to picnic sites, this area features eight or nine campsites, pit toilets, and put-ins for canoes and boats in the Potomac.

7

Historic Eastern Panhandle

HARPERS FERRY TO BERKELEY SPRINGS

GENERAL DESCRIPTION: From historic Harpers Ferry on the Potomac River, this 45-mile drive crosses the Shenandoah Valley to the resort mountain spa of Berkeley Springs.

SPECIAL ATTRACTIONS: Harpers Ferry National Historical Park, historical Shepherdstown, Martinsburg, Berkeley Springs State Park, the Shenandoah Valley, wooded mountain ridges.

LOCATION: Eastern-most West Virginia. Harpers Ferry is about 15 miles west of Frederick, Maryland, on US Highway 340, and about an hour's drive from Washington, D.C.

DRIVING ROUTE NUMBERS AND NAME: US 340, 522; WV 9, 45, 230.

TRAVEL SEASON: All year.

CAMPING: Primitive state campground in Sleepy Creek Wildlife Management Area west of Hedgesville. Private campgrounds near Harpers Ferry, and in Falling Waters 10 miles north of Martinsburg.

SERVICES: Gasoline, restaurants, and lodging are readily available in most towns.

NEARBY ATTRACTIONS: Harpers Ferry Toy Train Museum, Charles Town race tracks, Antietam National Battlefield Park, Chesapeake and Ohio Canal National Historic Park, Leetown National Fish Hatchery, Cacapon Resort State Park.

THE DRIVE

Jutting eastward from the body of the state, the cosmopolitan Eastern Panhandle lies closer to the nation's capitol and the Virginia and Maryland suburbs than it does to most of West Virginia. It doesn't look like a "panhandle" but that term is as descriptive of any of this peculiarly shaped region, cradled between Virginia and Maryland and bordered by the sinuous Potomac River along its northern and western edge.

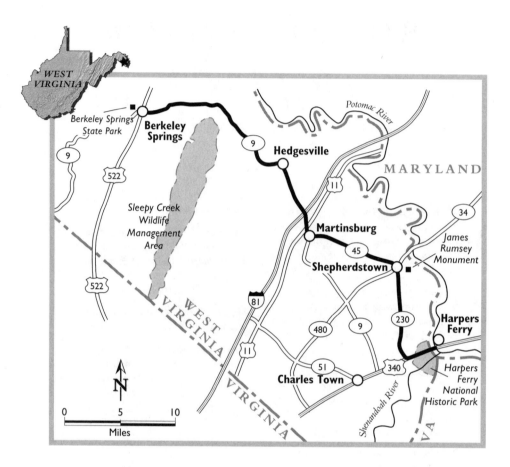

Harpers Ferry, the starting point and first stop for this 45-mile drive, is the eastern-most point in West Virginia. From here, the drive heads west through the Eastern Panhandle, crossing the West Virginia portion of the Shenandoah Valley farmlands, through the historic towns of Shepherdstown and Martinsburg. The drive then enters the Valley and Ridge province, climbing and descending several small ridges to end at the resorts and spas of Berkeley Springs.

The drive can easily be made in a few hours, but the many points of historic and scenic interest may spur you to linger along the way. If you don't make many stops, Drive 6, from Berkeley Springs to Paw Paw can be combined with this drive for a one-day trip.

This was the first part of West Virginia to be settled by Europeans. When most of the state was still an unknown mountain wilderness, the towns of Harpers Ferry, Shepherdstown, Martinsburg, and others had booming economies. Its proximity to the nation's capital has helped make it the fastest growing area of the state today, and one of the few regions that showed a population increase in the 2000 census.

History lies around virtually every bend. George Washington relaxed from his surveying duties to immerse his youthful body in the soothing natural spas of Berkeley Springs. The Civil War was born at Harpers Ferry after John Brown's failed raid to free the slaves focused the nation's attention on the moral issue of slavery. This led to West Virginia's succession from Virginia and admission to the Union in 1863. The steamboat was invented in Shepherdstown in 1787, some 20 years before Robert Fulton steamed up the Hudson River.

Three states—Virginia, West Virginia, and Maryland—and two rivers—the Potomac and the Shenandoah—come together at Harpers Ferry. Both rivers have cut yawning gaps through the Blue Ridge mountains; these passes have provided level travel routes east and west, by trail, railroad, canal, and road for more than 200 years. In fact, trains still stop here: a growing commuter community makes the daily hour-long trip back and forth to Washington, D.C.

The Blue Ridge itself continues south into Virginia; culminating in the much higher peaks along Skyline Drive in Shenandoah National Park and the Blue Ridge Parkway. These drives, plus some 20 others in the Old Dominion state, are described in the FalconGuide *Scenic Driving Virginia*, also published by The Globe Pequot Press.

The most picturesque approach to Harpers Ferry is from Frederick, Maryland, east of Harpers Ferry via US 340. This route descends into the Potomac River valley, crosses the river into Virginia, and a mile later crosses the Shenandoah River at its confluence with the Potomac to enter West Virginia. Both bridge crossings provide sweeping panoramas of the wide waterways and the steep and rocky slopes on either side; the Virginia portion has views across the Potomac to the town of Harpers Ferry, where buildings hug the flat ground along the river and climb step-like up the hillsides.

If you arrive from the other direction—from Charles Town, West Virginia on US 340—you'll reach Harpers Ferry before passing through the river valleys. So if you are coming from the west, before or after you visit Harpers Ferry follow US 340 east past the town for the views from the Shenandoah and Potomac river valleys.

Because parking is limited in Harpers Ferry, most motorists park at the Visitor Center on US 340 about a mile west of the historic area. There is a small entrance fee. From there, you can ride a free Park Service bus to the historic area.

HARPERS FERRY NATIONAL HISTORIC PARK

The town is named for John Harper who operated a ferry service across the two rivers in the mid 1700s. Today the town is contiguous with Harpers Ferry National Historic Park and has been restored to look much as it did in 1860 on the brink of the Civil War. Then it was a thriving rail and trade center with 3,000 residents, including an active community of 150 free blacks, many of whom were skilled and prosperous craftsmen such as masons and blacksmiths.

Many restored buildings now serve as small museums and exhibit areas; others are privately owned shops and restaurants. National Park Service programs show the interweaving and intertwined themes of history that have played a role here: the natural setting; the first major United States manufacturing center; the coming of the first successful railroad; John Brown's attack on slavery; the numerous Civil War battles; and the vital role of Storer College in educating former slaves in one of the earliest integrated schools in the country.

Several short hikes in this hilly town give you rewarding views for minimal effort, even though the town is only 280 feet above sea level and the lowest point in West Virginia. A five-minute stroll up the stone steps from High Street brings you to Jefferson Rock for a view that Thomas Jefferson declared was "worth a voyage across the Atlantic." Somewhat more strenuous is the Maryland Heights Trail, which gives you an outstanding view of the town and both rivers from the Maryland side of the Potomac.

The town is also headquarters for the Appalachian Trail Conference (ATC); the Appalachian Trail (AT) itself runs through the center of town. The trail, the world's best known hiking path, was built in bits and pieces starting in New Jersey in the 1920s. It was finally consolidated in 1951 into a 2100-mile footpath through 14 states from Springer Mountain, Georgia, to Mount Kathadin, Maine. The National Trails System Act in 1968 established the AT as a linear national park, officially known as the Appalachian National Scenic Trail. The Appalachian Trail Conference helps coordinate the many volunteer and governmental agencies that maintain the trail.

Harpers Ferry is about the mid-point of this elongated trek, and through hikers consider it an important milestone. Most stop by ATC

Harpers Ferry, now a historical national park, still bustles with activity after 300 years of history.

headquarters, the unofficial capital of the trail, to pay homage to the organization that helped to build the Appalachian Trail and continues to toil to maintain it.

Except for a few miles of the Appalachian Trail in the southern part of the state, this is the only section of the AT in West Virginia. South of Harpers Ferry the trail climbs past Jefferson Rock to the ridgeline border between Virginia and West Virginia. Northbound hikers follow the AT across the Potomac into Maryland, and along the Chesapeake and Ohio Canal for a few miles, where the trail turns north along low ridges into Pennsylvania.

Whitewater enthusiasts may enjoy a float or canoe trip down the Shenandoah Staircase, a six-mile stretch with several class I to III rapids. (I is mild; VI is the most advanced.). These waters are tame compared with the world class whitewater of West Virginia's New and Gauley rivers, but they are very well suited for family groups. Fishing, tubing, rafting, canoeing, and kayaking are popular on both rivers. Trips can be arranged through River and Trail Outfitters in nearby Knoxville, Maryland; call (301) 695-5177 for information and reservations.

How long you stay depends on your time and interests. Check with the Park Service for information on current activities and tours.

When you're ready to leave Harpers Ferry and do some actual driving, go north on US 340. About one mile past the visitor center, turn right on WV 230. (A few miles straight ahead on US 340 is Charles Town, surveyed by George Washington in 1747 and named for his younger brother. The town, often confused with the state capital, Charleston, has several restored Colonial buildings and is known for its race tracks: the Charles Town Race Track for thoroughbreds, and the Summit Point Raceway for sports car, Grand Prix, and motorcycle racing.)

WV 230 is a two-lane winding road that passes through the rolling farmland of the Shenandoah Valley. The rich limestone soil and gentle slopes help make this some of the most fertile land in the state, with abundant cattle ranches, truck farms, and peach and apple orchards.

As you cruise along you may want to burst into song and start harmonizing to the late John Denver's chart-breaking hit, "Country Roads." Denver wrote the song after a visit to the Eastern Panhandle. The first line, "Almost heaven, West Virginia," has become an internationally recognized symbol and icon for the state.

After 9 miles you reach Shepherdstown, on the banks of the Potomac River. Established in 1734 by Thomas Shepherd, the town was incorporated in 1762, and calls itself the oldest town in West Virginia. Many of the beautifully restored

Colonial homes and shops have helped place the town on the National Register of Historic Places. Most notable is the Entler Hotel, built in stages from 1786 to 1815, and now home to the Historic Shepherdstown Museum.

In the 1780s George Washington commissioned Shepherdstown resident James Rumsey to help develop and manage navigation on the Potomac River. But engineer Rumsey was more interested in building and inventing than he was in administration. In December 1787, his small steam-powered piston engine propelled a boat upstream in the turgid Potomac at the then astounding speed of three knots.

THE FIRST STEAMBOAT

Rumsey planned a larger, commercial version of his steamboat, but he died before this project could be floated. Some twenty years later Robert Fulton, building on Rumsey's design, cruised up the Hudson River in the first successful and commercially viable steamboat.

A replica of Rumsey's steamboat and other memorabilia of his life and work are on exhibit at the Rumsey Steamboat Museum behind the Entler Hotel. Several times each summer volunteers from the Rumseian Society fill the boilers, light the fire, and chug up and down the Potomac under a full head of steam.

The inventor is also memorialized at the James Rumsey Monument at the end of North Mill Street. This small park overlooks the Potomac from a 100-foot high bluff. The monument itself, a tall column topped with a globe of the earth, symbolizes the international importance of Rumsey's work.

The builder of the steamboat replica and a key member of the Rumseian Society is Jay O'Hurley, proprietor of O'Hurley's General Store. The store has been restored to look as it did in the early 1900s. Another town landmark is the Yellow Brick Bank Restaurant, a renovated 1900s-style bank; the former vault now houses the restaurant's extensive and presumably priceless wine cellar.

At the north end of town is the attractive campus of Shepherd College, the state's first liberal arts school, founded in 1872 and a center for the arts. Each July the college hosts the Contemporary American Theater Festival, during which presentations of new American plays are staged, plus dances, readings, and other offerings.

The town's bucolic atmosphere today belies its strife-riven history. During the Revolutionary War, Shepherdstown supplied more troops than any other town of its size. During the Civil War, shallows in the Potomac made Shepherdstown a strategic river crossing. The town served as a massive hospital following the Battle of Antietam (known to the Confederacy as the

The Rumsey Monument in Shepherdstown honors the inventor of the steamboat.

Battle of Sharpstown), on September 17, 1862, in Sharpstown, Maryland, five miles north of Shepherdstown.

THE BATTLE OF ANTIETAM

During this bloody one-day battle, Union General George McClellan's troops clashed with Confederate General Robert E. Lee's soldiers with more than 22,000 casualties. After the conflict Shepherdstown was filled with dead, dying, and injured men. Perhaps because of the unselfish care and attention the area's residents gave to soldiers of both sides, it was spared the burning and destruction that devastated so many other towns during the Civil War.

Although neither side claimed a victory in this battle, it dissuaded General Lee from moving farther north into federal territory; he withdrew to the south in what was considered a strategic victory for the federal forces.

WV 230 ends in Shepherdstown and becomes WV 45, which twists and winds its way for about 7 miles to Martinsburg. In the center of the West Virginia section of the Shenandoah Valley, Martinsburg has been an historic transportation, agricultural, and business center since colonial days.

Like Shepherdstown, the Martinsburg area was settled in the early 1700s. It soon became a hub for southern and western travelers who traversed the Valley Pike between Pennsylvania and Virginia. When the Baltimore and Ohio Railroad was built in the 1840s the town continued to thrive and prosper. The wagon and cart trails were succeeded by US 11 and I–81; the railroad remains, mostly as a freight line, but it maintains daily Amtrak and commuter service to Washington, D.C.

During the Civil War Martinsburg changed sides some sixty times, with widespread destruction throughout town. Despite the extensive damage, many beautiful eighteenth- and nineteenth-century buildings were preserved or have been restored.

The town today has seven historic districts and numerous buildings on the National Historic Register. You can obtain detailed information and maps for walking and driving tours at the Martinsburg/Berkeley County Convention and Visitors Bureau at the Boarman House at 208 South Queen Street. Upstairs from the visitor center is the Boarman House Arts Center, which emphasizes West Virginia artists.

Historic buildings of particular interest include the museum at the Belle Boyd House, the childhood home of the famous female Civil War spy, and the B&O Roundhouse, originally built in 1842 and destroyed nine times during the Civil War. The present roundhouse dates from 1868; a portion of it still functions as the Amtrak depot.

THE GEORGE WASHINGTON MEMORIAL TRAIL

To continue the drive turn west (right) on WV 9 at the T intersection of WV 45 and WV 9 in Martinsburg. Follow WV 9 west through Martinsburg, crossing US 11 and I–81. In a few minutes you're out in the dairy farms of the Shenandoah Valley. This 26-mile stretch from Martinsburg to Berkeley Springs is known as the George Washington Memorial Trail; it follows the historic turnpike first used by Native Americans and then by early settlers.

As you approach the small town of Hedgesville about 6 miles from Martinsburg, you climb a small hill and the road begins to gently curve. The hill, small by West Virginia standards, marks the boundary between the near-level Shenandoah Valley province and the much greater relief of the Ridge and Valley province.

Curves and hills continue past Hedgesville. Farms and pastures still cover most of the level ground but give way to mixed hardwood and pines on the steeper slopes, with higher tree-covered ridges in the distance that reach Maryland and Pennsylvania.

Young George Washington relaxed here in Berkeley Springs after a long day of surveying.

After a few miles you pass the entrance to The Woods, known for its golfing and retirement community, and one of the many resorts in the area. For those who want a more rustic setting, nearby is the state-run Sleepy Creek Wildlife Management Area, where a primitive campground for hunters and fishermen nestles on a 205-acre lake in a verdant valley between twin ridges.

Several more curves and bends past the nose of Sleepy Creek Mountain bring you to end of the drive at the resort town of Berkeley Springs and Berkeley Springs State Park at the intersection of US 522. The area has been known for its spas and mineral baths since the first Native Americans sought relaxation here more than 300 years ago. George Washington surveyed the town as a young man. He so much enjoyed soaking in the warm waters that he bought property in town, and for more than forty years—even while president—he returned here for relaxation. He also named the town Bath after the English spa, which is still the legal name of the town today.

Bathing in the springs is still a prime attraction here, but shopping and sightseeing are also popular. The town is the beginning of Drive 6, Berkeley Springs to Paw Paw; that drive describes the town and area. Please read the material there to learn more about Berkeley Springs, even if you don't plan to continue on that drive.

8

ceɳter state Raᴍᵬle

A COVERED BRIDGE, THE WILDLIFE CENTER, AND HISTORIC HELVETIA

GENERAL DESCRIPTION: A 71-mile drive on paved roads through the gentle hills of central West Virginia. It features unspoiled small college towns, the West Virginia State Wildlife Center, and the historic town of Helvetia.

SPECIAL ATTRACTIONS: The Philippi covered bridge and mummies, the West Virginia State Wildlife Center, and the Swiss town of Helvetia.

LOCATION: Central West Virginia, almost in the middle of the state, beginning at Philippi.

DRIVING ROUTE NUMBERS AND NAME: US 119; WV 11, 20, 46.

TRAVEL SEASON: All year, but some attractions may be closed or have reduced hours in winter. Heavy winter snow may close roads temporarily.

CAMPING: No camping along the drive itself, but nearby state parks have full-service camping facilities, including Holly River, Audra, Stonewall Jackson Lake, and Tygart Lake state parks, for a total of more than 200 campsites. Buckhannon has several private campgrounds.

SERVICES: All services are available in Philippi and Buckhannon. Gas is not available past Buckhannon, and lodging and restaurants are limited.

NEARBY ATTRACTIONS: The state parks mentioned above all have swimming and fishing facilities and hiking trails. Grafton, north of Philippi, has a shrine to Anna Jarvis, the mother of Mother's Day, and her birthplace is a few miles south of Grafton toward Philippi.

THE DRIVE

The small towns of central West Virginia have a charm that reflects their pastoral location, friendly residents, and easy living. This 71-mile drive starts near the covered bridge and mummies of Philippi. You then head south to Buckhannon, home of West Virginia Wesleyan College, and continue to French Creek to view the bison, elk, and river otters of the West Virginia State Wildlife Center. From there it's through unspoiled woods and hills to Helvetia, restored

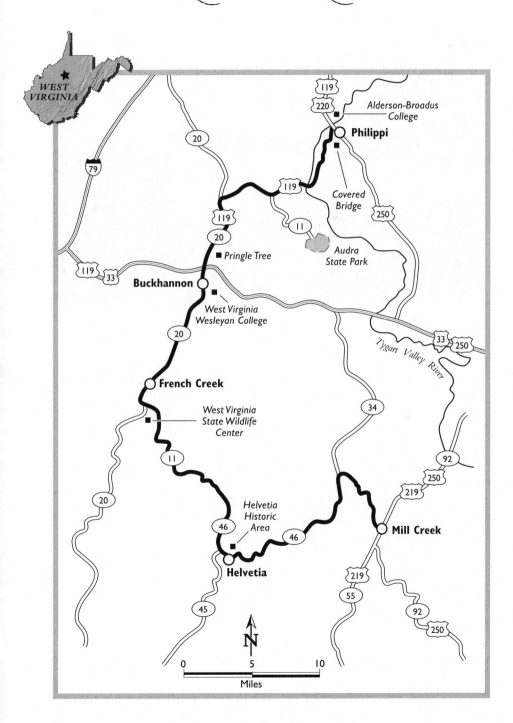

WEST VIRGINIA

119
220
Alderson-Broadus College
Philippi
20
79
119
Covered Bridge
250
119
20
11
Audra State Park
Pringle Tree
119
33
Buckhannon
West Virginia Wesleyan College
20
33
250
Tygart Valley River
French Creek
West Virginia State Wildlife Center
34
92
11
250
219
20
Helvetia Historic Area
46
46
Mill Creek
Helvetia
219
45
55
92
250

N

0   5   10
Miles

Route 250 spans the Tygart Valley River in Philippi through the only covered bridge in the country to serve a U.S. highway.

to look as it did when settled by Swiss immigrants in 1869. The drive gets a little bit more rugged beyond Helvetia, but with views to match the hills and curves, and ends at Mill Creek. All roads are paved two-lane.

This is a long drive with lots to see and do. You can easily spend several hours at the Wildlife Center and in Helvetia. You may want to visit Philippi and Buckhannon and stay overnight in Buckhannon, the only place on the drive where motels are plentiful, for a two-day trip.

Philippi is perhaps best known for its covered bridge, the longest and oldest in the state. Built in 1852, this handsome, 285-foot structure was designed by Lemuel Chenoweth. His improved Burr Arch Truss model was widely admired and frequently copied by other bridge builders. The bridge, almost in downtown Philippi, spans the Tygart Valley River and is the country's only two-lane covered bridge that serves a U.S. highway (US 250). Chenoweth also designed the Barrackville covered bridge, which is still standing but not open to vehicular traffic.

Nine years after construction, on March 6, 1861, the Philippi bridge was the site of the first land battle of the Civil War when Union soldiers confronted Confederate troops in a minor battle. There were no casualties in this encounter, but the Confederates retreated so swiftly that the skirmish is often referred to as "the Philippi Races."

Among the few wounded in the battle was a Confederate soldier, James Hanger, whose leg had to be amputated after it was crushed by cannon shot. Hanger was not content to spend the rest of his life hobbling around on one leg, so he fashioned himself an artificial wooden one. His workmanship so impressed the Confederate brass that they contracted with Hanger to provide artificial limbs for other wounded soldiers, a job that kept him busy for several years. After the war Hanger formed a company to continue manufacturing prostheses; that corporation is still in business today and is listed on the New York Stock Exchange.

Chenoweth's bridge survived the battle plus several floods and fires over the years, but a fire in 1989 almost destroyed it. Using Chenoweth's original plans, the bridge was carefully restored and rebuilt. Today it maintains its original appearance, including the yellow poplar exterior, and is still structurally sound for modern usage.

THE MUMMIES OF PHILIPPI

You can learn more about the bridge and the Civil War battle in the Barbour County Historical Museum, across the street from the bridge in a restored 1911 railroad depot. But many visitors to the museum are more interested in its one hundred-year-old residents, the Philippi mummies. The mummies are two unnamed females who previously resided in what was then the Hospital for the Insane in nearby Weston. After their death in 1888, their bodies were obtained by Graham Hamrick, a local resident and part-time undertaker. Hamrick had invented a mummification process that he had already applied successfully to squirrels and vegetables.

The two corpses gave Hamrick the opportunity to apply his preservative methods to humans. He was so pleased with the results that he applied for and was granted a patent for the mummification process. For their part the ladies went on a worldwide tour as the Hamrick Mummies with P.T. Barnum in 1891. They then returned to Philippi, where they were exhibited sporadically and rested in obscurity.

On the bluff to the north of town is the campus of Alderson-Broadus College, a leading school for the training of physicians' assistants and other paramedical personnel. Downtown Philippi has several historical buildings, most notably the imposing Barbour County Courthouse.

From Philippi drive south on US 119 through gently rolling farmland and woods. Relief here is low, with no major grades or curves. Nearby is Audra State Park, a favorite place for picnicking, swimming, and sunbathing.

AT HOME IN THE PRINGLE TREE

US 119 is joined by WV 20. Continue south (left) on US 119/WV 20. About 18 miles from Philippi look for signs to the Pringle Tree. Just off the highway to the left, the current tree is the third generation descendant of a huge, hollow sycamore that served as home and refuge for two brothers, John and Samuel Pringle. The brothers deserted from the British Army at Fort Pitt (Pittsburgh) in 1761, and when they found the hollow tree in the wilderness, they settled there, living on game and forage. Reputedly their living quarters in the hollow trunk were a room more than 11 feet wide.

Several years later, when they learned the war was over, they returned to civilization. Their enthusiasm for the area helped attract permanent settlers to this then far-western region. The sycamore at the site today is a scant reminder of the giant sycamores that once were found across the state.

The town of Buckhannon is about 1 mile past the Pringle Tree. To continue on the drive, cross under US 33 and continue south on WV 20. (US 119 turns west on US 33.) You may want to take a few moments in Buckhannon to visit the picturesque, hundred-year-old tree-shaded Georgian-style campus of West Virginian Wesleyan College. At the campus center is the Wesley Chapel, easily spotted by its imposing steeple. With 1,600 seats the chapel is the largest in the state; its huge organ with 1,500 pipes is easily heard from all seats. Also on campus is the Sleeth Art Gallery.

In May, to top off the local harvest, Buckhannon celebrates the week-long Strawberry Festival. In addition to the eats—strawberries, strawberries with cream, strawberry cobbler, strawberry pie, and more strawberries—the Strawberry Queen leads the parade down Strawberry Lane. Call the Chamber of Commerce (see Appendix) for exact dates and more information.

As you leave town on WV 20, you pass numerous well-maintained Victorian style mansions interspersed with moderate suburban sprawl. Opposite a supermarket and easy to miss is the Little Hungary Farm Winery, about 1 mile past US 33. The winery is renowned for its Melomel, a fruity Hungarian mixture of apples, pears, grapes, and honey.

THE STATE WILDLIFE CENTER

At French Creek, about 12 miles from Buckhannon, turn left on WV 11 at the well-marked entrance to the West Virginia State Wildlife Center. The facility, operated by the West Virginia Division of Natural Resources, displays native and introduced wildlife of the state in 300 acres of woods and meadows. Mountain lions, timber wolves, black bear, deer, and other animals may be viewed in natural habitats. A special river otter exhibit lets you see the animals from both above and below the water. Animals no longer found in West Virginia, such as bison and elk, graze in open fields. A 1.25-mile loop walking trail passes by most of the exhibits.

The center was originally opened as a game farm in 1923. As conservationist thinking changed, the idea of a game farm went out of favor, and the current wildlife center and philosophy were established in 1986. You can visit any time, but a nominal admission fee is charged from April 1 to October 31 when the visitor center is open.

When you leave the parking lot for the center, turn right (east) on WV 11. The 20 miles to Helvetia are less settled and more hilly and curvy than the first part of the drive, past farms, open fields, and thick woods with groves of rhododendron. You'll also pass the pipes and well heads of several gas wells. As you cross from Upshur County to Randolph County, the route number changes to WV 46.

SWITZERLAND IN WEST VIRGINIA

Helvetia is a little bit of Switzerland preserved and hidden in the hills of West Virginia. The town was settled in 1869 by Swiss immigrants and soon became a bustling farm community of about 1,000 folks. They named their town Helvetia, the Latin term for Switzerland.

Today there are only about 200 residents, but the Swiss pride and heritage live on. Through their efforts some ten historic buildings have been preserved, and the entire village has been placed on the National Register of Historic Places. The buildings include the original one-room schoolhouse, a settler's cabin that is now a museum, a small inn, a church, and a library. The buildings, clustered along the banks of a gurgling stream, can be visited with a minimum of walking. Entrance to all buildings is free. The museum is open on Sundays during the warmer months.

The townspeople also honor their heritage with song, dance, and frivolity. The Helvetia Fair, held during the second weekend in September, celebrates the harvest with a cheese festival and animal parade; Fasnacht, the Saturday before Ash Wednesday, memorializes the end of winter when everybody dresses in costume and Old Man Winter is burned in effigy.

If you're feeling hungry, the Hütte restaurant, under the direction of town historian, preservationist, and chef Eleanor Mailloux, serves local food pre-

The entire village of Helvetia is on the National Register of Historic Places.

pared in genuine Swiss style. If you're lucky enough to be there for Sunday brunch or lunch, be sure to order the Bernerplatte, a bountiful buffet of Swiss culinary masterpieces. Dishes, all homemade, include Stout soup, sausage, sauerkraut, sauerbraten, Helvetian Swiss cheese, and a tasty variety of breads and desserts. But be forewarned: This is the only restaurant for miles around, and it is popular.

When you leave town, continue east on WV 46. This section of the drive is the most rugged, as the topography soon changes, with higher hills, steeper grades, and more curves. The hills soon turn into distinct ridges, with distant views from the high points. At the bottom of one valley is a coal mine and loading station on a railroad spur.

The drive concludes about 21 miles from Helvetia with a steep descent to the junction with US 219/250 in the town of Mill Creek along the Tygart Valley River.

9

caŋaaŋ Valley Loop

THROUGH THE STATE'S HIGHEST VALLEY

GENERAL DESCRIPTION: A 45-mile loop drive in the Monongahela National Forest through the mountains and wetlands of Canaan Valley, the highest valley of its size east of the Rockies.

SPECIAL ATTRACTIONS: Canaan Valley Resort State Park, Canaan Valley National Wildlife Refuge, and Blackwater Falls State Park.

LOCATION: East-central West Virginia, south of Morgantown.

DRIVING ROUTE NUMBERS AND NAME: US 219, WV 32, 72.

TRAVEL SEASON: All year. Snows are heavy in winter; WV 72 may be closed temporarily. Many attractions are seasonal.

CAMPING: Canaan Valley Resort State Park is open all year and has thirty-four tent or trailer sites with all facilities. Blackwater Falls State Park is open May through November and has sixty-five tent or trailer sites, about half with all facilities.

SERVICES: Food and fuel are available year-round in Davis and along WV 32 and US 219. Motels, ski resorts, condominiums, and lodges in the state parks provide numerous overnight accommodations year-round. Reservations are recommended, particularly during ski season and when fall foliage is at its peak. There are no services along WV 72.

NEARBY ATTRACTIONS: Fairfax Stone and Dolly Sods.

THE DRIVE

Canaan (pronounced Ka NEEN) Valley is the highest valley of its size east of the Rockies and the largest wetland complex in West Virginia. Surrounded by mountains, its diverse habitats include dense deciduous and conifer forests, swiftly flowing streams and waterfalls, and fragile bogs and wetlands.

Within the valley are found almost 300 species of birds, mammals, fishes, reptiles, and amphibians, and about 600 species of plants. Rimmed by mountains, the bowl-like valley receives 150 to 200 inches of snow each year, and with an average elevation of 3,200 feet, its climate is more like parts of New England than most of West Virginia.

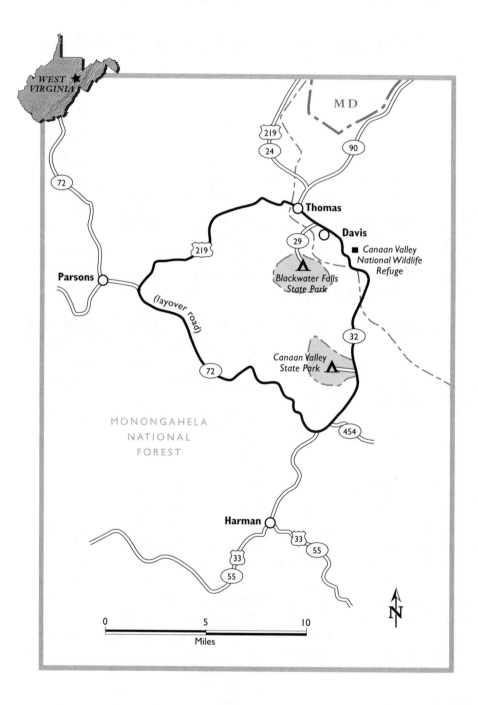

With all this going for it, it's not surprising that the valley is a four-season destination. Within its bounds can be found two state parks, a national wildlife refuge, and numerous ski resorts and condos. Popular activities include skiing, hiking, birding, golfing, sightseeing, and just plain relaxing.

The valley was named "Canaan" by settlers in the 1700s who thought they had found a piece of the biblical promised land in the New World. It was little known until the 1850s, when the name and the valley were popularized by author and illustrator David Hunter Strother, better known by his pen name of Porte Crayon. His series of writings and drawings of the mountains of West Virginia in *Harper's New Monthly Magazine* made him the most celebrated travel writer of his time.

This loop drive can be started from several entry points and driven in either direction. As described here it begins at the southern tip of the loop at the intersection of WV 32 and 72. It follows WV 32 north about 15 miles through the center of the valley to Davis and Blackwater Falls State Park. At Thomas the drive turns west on US 219 for 12 miles to WV 72, outside the town of Parsons. From here it is an 18-mile drive south on little-traveled and narrow WV 72 through high country west of the valley to the starting point at WV 32. This totals about 45 miles, but you will add some for trips off the main drive. The entire drive lies within the authorized boundary of the Monongahela National Forest.

From the starting point drive north on WV 32 through an open valley almost surrounded by mountains. After a few miles you come to the entrance of Canaan Valley Resort State Park, one of the state's premier resort parks, developed for year-round use. In winter skiers ride chairlifts to the mountaintops and schuss down on skis over groomed, steep slopes. Cross-country skiers and snowshoers can glide through the quiet forests on several miles of trails. Après-ski activities include soothing sore muscles in the hot tubs at the health spa, swimming in the indoor pool, or just relaxing in the modern lodge.

THE WALK BETWEEN THE PARKS

When the snow melts and the wildflowers start to bloom, the cross-country trails turn into hiking trails. The wheelchair-accessible Abe Run Boardwalk gives virtually all visitors a chance to see deer, beaver, swamp sparrows, cedar waxwings, and perhaps a muskrat. A popular day trip is the "Walk Between the Parks," an 8.5-mile one-way hike to Blackwater Falls State Park. Other hikes connect to the trail system in the adjoining Monongahela National Forest.

The warmer months bring a variety of scheduled activities, from wildflower pilgrimages to bird watching to astronomy weekends during the park's dark nights. Stop at the nature center to find out what is currently offered. Golfers can indulge in scenic driving of another sort at the championship eighteen-hole course, followed by a dip in the outdoor Olympic-sized swimming pool.

When you're ready to leave the state park, return to WV 32 and turn north (left). Several roads to the right lead to private ski resorts, and you will see numerous signs for condominiums. Also off to the right are the high marshes, wetlands, and high country of the Canaan Valley National Wildlife Refuge, with flora and ecology that more nearly resemble Canada than most of West Virginia.

Established in 1994 as the country's 500th national wildlife refuge, its 6,700 acres protect numerous plant communities that have survived in these high elevation marshes since the end of the Pleistocene ice age. In addition to having some 600 species of plants, each spring and fall these marshes—the second largest freshwater wetlands in the United States—provide feeding grounds for enormous numbers of migrating wading birds, shorebirds, and waterfowl. It is also a major breeding area for the American woodcock.

Development has been minimal, and most visitors must seek out the few unmarked trails. You can plan your visit in advance by calling or contacting the refuge (see the Appendix). One popular trail begins on Freeland Road near the White Grass Ski Touring Center; another starts from Old Timberline Road near Cortland. None of these roads is shown on the map in this book; ask locally for detailed directions.

Continue on WV 32 to the town of Davis, about 15 miles from the starting point. At an elevation of about 3,000 feet, Davis is the highest incorporated town east of the Mississippi; its wide streets and wooden false fronts on many buildings help to give it a Western look. Natural air conditioning made it popular as a summer resort more than a hundred years ago. It's even more popular today, all year long, with skiers, hikers, golfers, anglers, fall foliage viewers, and others who find respite and relaxation in the colorful cafes, restaurants, galleries, and craft shops.

BLACKWATER FALLS AND GORGE

Just outside town on the left is a main reason people come to Davis: Blackwater Falls State Park. The crown jewel of the park, Blackwater Falls, careens and cascades more than 60 feet into the 8-mile-long gorge of the Blackwater River.

The world first learned about Blackwater Falls from the vivid descriptions and sketches by Porte Crayon. Reaching the falls in his day was an arduous and difficult trip afoot or on horseback on poorly defined trails over rugged

The Blackwater River cascades over the rocks.

hills and canyons covered with rhododendron, hemlock, red spruce, and hardwood trees.

Today the falls, known by Crayon as the Great Falls of the Blackwater, are accessible via a wooden boardwalk. As you descend the numerous steps, the roar of the water grows louder at every viewpoint, reaching a crescendo at the base of the falls. Here you can look up at the cascade of water as it pours and tumbles over the rocks.

Beyond the falls the Blackwater River roars through an 8-mile canyon. The river gets its name from the tannic acid and iron leached from decaying vegetation, mostly hemlock leaves and red spruce needles, that give it its characteristic tea-colored hue.

Other hiking trails wind through the thick woods, including the "Walk Between the Parks" back to Canaan Valley State Park. Most popular and easiest is the paved, wheelchair-accessible Gentle Trail, which leads to an observation deck overlooking the falls. More severe is the undeveloped Blackwater Canyon Rail Trail that traverses the gorge along an old narrow gauge logging railroad. Winter brings a quiet solitude of green and white as heavy snows cover the trails, and the park becomes a ski-touring center. A well-equipped ski shop provides equipment and rentals.

Canaan Valley Loop

A mountain hike in Canaan Valley Resort State Park passes a small lake.
Photo: Stephen J. Shalnta Jr., courtesy West Virginia Division of Tourism.

Open all year, the lodge and restaurant offer diners and overnight guests scenic views into the canyon. A variety of year-round nature programs, guided hikes, and other events, such as the Septemberfest Senior Fling, may add interest to your visit. A campsite is open during the warmer months.

When you return to WV 32, continue north (left). At the intersection in Thomas, turn left again (west) on US 219, a wide, two-lane major highway. This section of US 219 follows part of the Seneca Trail or Warriors Path, a Native American footpath from what is now New York to the south. Efforts are being made to preserve parts of the path before it is swallowed up by development. A roadside rest area at the top of a ridge provides a panoramic view.

About 8 miles from Thomas begins a 4-mile downgrade to the Cheat River Valley and the intersection with WV 72. Turn south (left) on WV 72. There are no services along WV 72, so if you need gas or food, stay on US 219 another mile to the town of Parsons, then backtrack to WV 72. In addition, although it is paved, portions of WV 72 are very narrow, hilly, and winding, and are not suited for trailers or large RVs.

A LAYOVER ROAD

For a few miles WV 72 borders a popular fishing creek and passes several small communities. The road becomes so narrow that in places the paved portion is not wide enough for two vehicles to pass. This is known in West Virginia as a "layover road." This means that when you encounter an oncoming vehicle, both of you will pull over—layover—to the right as far as possible. The left wheels of both vehicles will be on the paved portion; the right wheels will be in the dirt. This is the layover position, and the two of you can safely pass. It is considered good manners to wave to the other driver as you go by.

After a few miles the road becomes very twisty and climbs steeply from the creek. The heavy woods give way to numerous open fields and grazing lands, too steep for farming. After passing the small settlement of Red Creek, both WV 72 and the drive end at the junction with WV 32 at the starting point.

Through Greenland Gap

MOOREFIELD TO SCHEER

GENERAL DESCRIPTION: A 22-mile drive along a pleasant river valley, a gentle mountain ridge, and through the towering cliffs of Greenland Gap.

SPECIAL ATTRACTIONS: Greenland Gap's cliffs, birds, and other wildlife, the Moorefield historic district, and the wide valley of the South Branch of the Potomac River.

LOCATION: East central West Virginia.

DRIVING ROUTE NUMBERS AND NAME: US 220/WV 28; WV 1, 2, 3, 3–3, 5.

TRAVEL SEASON: All year. Migrating birds are best seen in Greenland Gap in early

May and after cold fronts pass through in autumn. Rhododendrons reach their peak in July. Winter has a unique charm in Greenland Gap, but travel may be restricted for a day or two after snowstorms.

CAMPING: None.

SERVICES: All services are available in Moorefield.

NEARBY ATTRACTIONS: Spruce Knob, Dolly Sods, Seneca Rocks, and the Potomac Eagle excursion train in Romney.

THE DRIVE

This short drive heads northeast from Moorefield along the valley of the South Branch of the Potomac River. It then climbs the gentle slopes of Patterson Creek Mountain and passes through the nature preserve and clefts of Greenland Gap to end at the little town of Scheer.

Moorefield, like many towns in eastern West Virginia, changed hands numerous times during the Civil War. The historic district preserves several old buildings, as well as the home of Dr. H. M. Gamble, a physician and botanist. Dr. Gamble founded the West Virginia Medical Society, but he is equally revered for his botanical achievements; his extensive collection of native plants helped establish the West Virginia Herbarium at the West Virginia University in Morgantown.

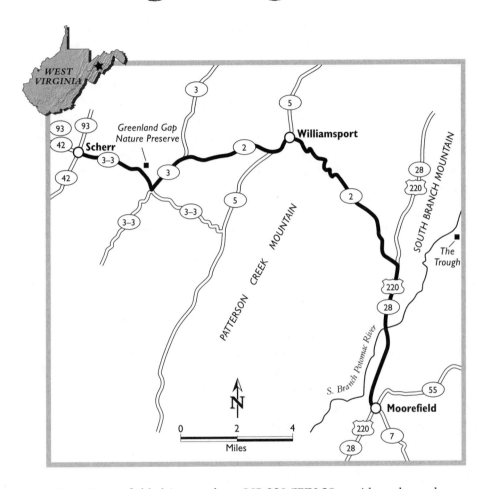

WEST VIRGINIA

3

5

93 93 Greenland Gap
Nature Preserve
42 Scherr 2 Williamsport
3-3
3
42

5
3-3

3-3

28
220

PATTERSON CREEK MOUNTAIN

SOUTH BRANCH MOUNTAIN

2

The
Trough

220

28

S. Branch Potomac River

55

N

Moorefield

0 2 4

220 7

Miles

28

From Moorefield, drive north on US 220/WV 28, a wide and paved two-lane road. This takes you along the broad, open valley of the South Branch of the Potomac River past prosperous dairy farms. This pastoral scene is framed by low-lying mountain ridges on both sides: To the northeast (right) is South Branch Mountain; to the northwest (left) is Patterson Creek Mountain, which you will cross in a few miles.

As you look ahead you can see where the South Branch of the Potomac in its northward journey narrows as it flows through Falling Springs Gap. The other side of this gap marks the beginning of The Trough, a steep and picturesque river canyon known for its bald eagle nesting sites. You can tour the canyon from the popular Potomac Eagle Scenic Railroad, which departs from Romney. The trains run during the warmer months, and eagles are seen on almost every trip.

After crossing the South Branch of the Potomac, turn left (west) on Old Fields Road (WV 2), near the small post office about 5 miles from Moorefield. This narrow, two-lane paved road rambles across the undulating limestone plains of the wide valley. After a few miles it climbs the gentle slopes of Patterson Creek Mountain past open fields of grazing cattle and sheep.

A moderate descent down the other side ends at the stop sign in Williamsport at WV 5. Turn left (south). Go about three-quarters of a mile to Belle Babb Lane, a continuation of WV 2, and turn right (west). You will pass a 30-foot-high earthen embankment that was built for flood control along the North Fork of Patterson Creek, the stream that flows through Greenland Gap.

At the stop sign and fork in the road, about 17.5 miles from the start of the drive, bear left (south) on WV 5. A half a mile down that road lies Greenland Gap Road (WV 3–3) and the entrance to Greenland Gap Nature Preserve; turn right.

INTO GREENLAND GAP

Greenland Gap is one of several passes or gaps through Knobly Mountain. The rocks here are intensely folded, and the ridge itself is made up of the Tuscarora sandstone of the Silurian age. Because the sandstone is resistant to weathering, most of the ridges and mountain tops are underlain by sandstone rock, and the Tuscarora sandstone is one of the major ridge-formers throughout the Appalachian Mountains.

As you enter the preserve, open fields give way to thick woods covered with dense thickets of rhododendron, which burst into colorful blossoms in July. Rhododendrons grow best in acid soils that develop in areas underlain by sandstone, and the plant's abundance here gives a clue to the underlying rock. Almost immediately the drive squeezes past the rapids at Falls Gap, a pleasant introduction to the featured attraction just ahead. At Falls Gap the clear waters of the North Fork gurgle and tumble down the steeply inclined bedrock.

A half-mile farther on at the small parking area at the main gap, cliffs of Tuscarora sandstone rise 800 feet above the creek on either side. Along the road are huge blocks of sandstone fallen from the cliffs above. Several trailheads lead off along the river; for a more strenuous hike, follow the trail to the top of the cliffs.

Water tumbles down the slope of the rocks at Falls Gap.

Turkey vultures nest on the steep cliffs above Greenland Gap.

Greenland Gap is one of twenty-four nature preserves maintained by the West Virginia chapter of the Nature Conservancy. The cliff tops of this 250-acre preserve make superb viewing points to observe migrating neotropical birds flying north in early May. The autumn migration is more drawn out in time, and the best viewing opportunities often follow cold fronts. In warm weather turkey vultures soar lazily overhead on the strong updrafts from the cliffs; the rocky crags make this an ideal place for these birds to lay their eggs. If you wander through the woods you may spot some white-tailed deer, wild turkeys, or even a black bear. Greenland Gap Nature Preserve is open all year. Snow may temporarily close the road in winter.

When you leave the preserve, bear left on WV 1 in the hamlet of Greenland. You'll pass several limestone quarries operated by the State Road Commission for road fill. At the stop sign in Scheer, bear left and go 500 feet to WV 93 and the end of the drive. To return to Moorefield turn around and retrace your trip, or turn left on WV 93 to go to Petersburg and then Moorefield.

11

Lost River and Cacapon River

CLEAR STREAMS AND GENTLE MOUNTAINS

GENERAL DESCRIPTION: A 55-mile drive that meanders along the headwaters of two crystal-clear streams through gentle mountains adjacent to the George Washington National Forest.

SPECIAL ATTRACTIONS: Lost River State Park, Capon Springs Resort, scenic river valleys, and rolling farmlands.

LOCATION: Eastern West Virginia, about 20 miles west of Winchester and Front Royal, Virginia, and I-81.

DRIVING ROUTE NUMBERS AND NAME: WV 12, 14, 16, 55, 259.

TRAVEL SEASON: All year.

CAMPING: The campground at Edward's Run Wildlife Management Area north of Capon Bridge has a few year-round primitive sites. The George Washington National Forest seasonally maintains the Hawk Campground Area near Capon Springs and Trout Pond Campground near Lost River. A private campground adjoins Lost River State Park and is open seasonally.

SERVICES: All services are available in most towns along the drive.

NEARBY ATTRACTIONS: George Washington National Forest and Potomac Eagle Scenic Railroad.

THE DRIVE

Compared to the rugged ridges and crags of Seneca Rocks, Spruce Peak, and Dolly Sods, the northeastern section of the Potomac Highlands is a land of gentle mountains and placid streams. Farms and villages, forests and small towns, and brooks and hills create a variety of tranquil scenery that is a delight to the eye and a balm to the mind.

This drive explores the headwaters of two of the region's scenic waterways, the Cacapon and Lost Rivers. You'll pass a historic spa, traverse a short but narrow canyon, and have almost constant views of distant mountains. The

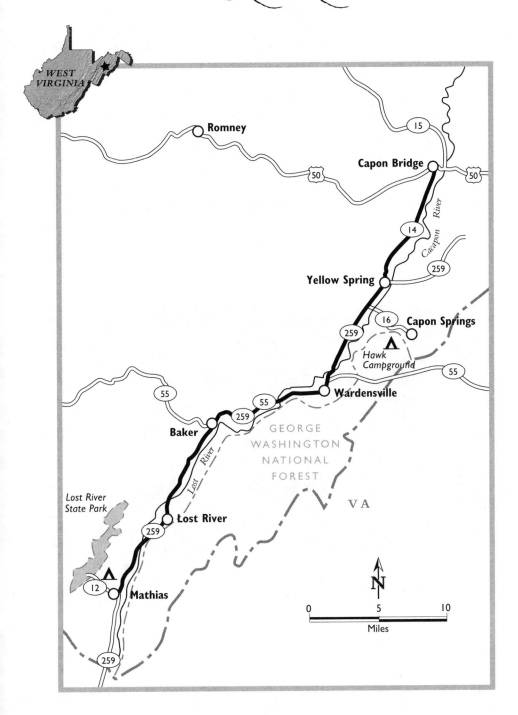

drive ends at one of West Virginia's outstanding state parks. Only two hours from the Washington, D.C., metropolitan area, the drive can easily be made as part of a day trip for urban dwellers.

The drive begins at the bridge in the town of Capon Bridge, about halfway between Winchester, Virginia, and Romney, West Virginia. Go south on WV 14, Cacapon River Road, just west of the iron truss bridge across the river on US 50.

At the first farm outside town on the left, look for fields with herds of llamas, bison, burros, miniature horses, and a flock of ostrich-like emus. Although this is private property, the animals are easily visible from the road.

The route follows the clear-flowing Cacapon River, popular with anglers for its largemouth and smallmouth bass and catfish. Numerous fishing camps line both sides of the river. Where the valley is wider, the flat floodplain along the river is used by grazing cattle and sheep or to grow hay and corn. The steep ridge to the right is Cacapon Mountain. As the drive heads upstream to the headwaters of the Cacapon, the river gradually narrows.

At the intersection in Yellow Spring, about 10 miles from Capon Bridge, WV 14 ends. Bear right (south) on WV 259. Two miles beyond that, an old

Llamas and emus on a farm near the Cacapon River.

highway bridge is partially preserved as a fishing pier. Just past the old bridge, turn left (east) on WV 16, Capon Springs Road. (The name "Capon" has nothing to do with altered chickens; it is a shortened version of "Cacapon," the American Indian name for the river.)

CAPON SPRINGS RESORT

WV 16 leaves the Cacapon River to wind along a small creek through thick woods to the small settlement at Capon Springs. Continue straight at the intersection by the octagon house to reach the historic district, springs, and resort. (To the right is the Hawk Campground in the George Washington National Forest.)

The springs here were known to the American Indians and attracted European settlers in the late 1700s. Gradually a resort developed, and in 1849 a four-story hotel was built to cater to the well-to-do who came here to enjoy the carbonated-lithium spring waters. The hotel burned down in 1911.

The graceful Victorian-style buildings that line both sides of the main street today were built in the 1880s. Now a national registered historic district, they serve a family-oriented resort known for its home cooking and casual atmosphere. The former bathhouses have been converted to residences, but the large main pool remains.

This 1880 Victorian hotel at Capon Springs still serves guests.

When you leave Capon Springs, turn around, go back to WV 259, and turn south (left), leaving the Cacapon watershed. After a few miles the valley opens up with distant views of mountains to the east. At the intersection with WV 55, bear south and west (right) on WV 55/259.

Past Wardensville, cross a small ridge that divides the watershed of the Cacapon River from that of Lost River. After a short drive downhill you enter the picturesque gorge at the headwaters of Lost River. The river gets its name because it gets "lost" as it flows through a cave for several hundred feet. Some say that the underground river connects the Cacapon and Lost Rivers. As you emerge from the gorge, note the old quarry where you can see the near-vertical beds of sandstone and limestone that were intensely folded during mountain building 250 million years ago.

At Baker turn left (south) on WV 259 where WV 55 continues straight. Lost River here flows through a flat valley, bordered abruptly on the left by steep wooded hills that mark the approximate boundary of the George Washington National Forest.

As you progress downstream the valley widens. The "Lost" theme continues as you pass through the small communities of Lost River and Lost City. Look for the sign to Lost River State Park just before Mathias. At the turn is the restored John Mathias Homestead, a log cabin built in 1797.

A restoration of John Mathias's homestead, originally built in 1797.

ON TO LOST RIVER

Turn right on WV 12 for a 4-mile drive to the wooded and hilly park. Most of Lost River State Park originally was the property of General Henry "Light Horse Harry" Lee, father of Confederate General Robert E. Lee. The elder Lee received the land as a grant for his military leadership during the Revolutionary War. He built a cabin by Howard's Lick, a sulphuric spring, also known as Lee White Sulphur Spring. Several horseback and hiking trails now lead to the cabin and spring.

Other trails in the park lead to scenic overlooks, including 3,200-foot-high Cranny Crow Overlook, with commanding views of surrounding ridges. The park, including several rental cottages, is open year-round. Seasonal activities include naturalist programs, a riding stable, swimming, and a restaurant and gift shop. A private campground adjacent to the park is available during the warmer months.

The drive ends at the park. You can retrace your route, follow the signs to go to Moorefield, or return to Mathias and follow WV 259 south to New Market, Virginia, and I–81.

12

Dolly Sods Scenic Area

ON TOP OF THE ALLEGHENY FRONT

GENERAL DESCRIPTION: This 30-mile drive within Monongahela National Forest climbs 2,500 feet up the steep Allegheny Front on a dirt road to magnificent views at the Dolly Sods, a windswept high plain with a climate and flora similar to northern Canada.

SPECIAL ATTRACTIONS: The Allegheny Front, the highland plain, unusual plants, one-sided spruces, unsurpassed 50-mile scenic views, walks and hikes, and migrating hawks and other birds.

LOCATION: The Potomac Highlands of eastern West Virginia about 10 miles west of Petersburg.

DRIVING ROUTE NUMBERS AND NAME: WV 45–4; FS 19, 75.

TRAVEL SEASON: Spring through autumn, but watch the weather. Severe thunderstorms, gale-force winds, and thick fog can move in quickly. Snow can occur any time from early autumn to late spring, and the

road is not plowed. Check with the Forest Service if you have any doubts about conditions or the weather. Migrating songbirds and hawks are best viewed from mid-August through mid-October.

CAMPING: The Red Creek Campground has twelve primitive sites with pit toilets. Canaan Valley State Park (Drive 9) near the northern end of the drive has about thirty-five fully equipped campsites. Seneca Shadows Campground, 1 mile south of Seneca Rocks, has about eighty campsites.

SERVICES: None. Make sure you have enough gas. If you want, bring a lunch to picnic at the Red Creek Campground picnic site.

NEARBY ATTRACTIONS: The drive lies in the middle of some of the most superb scenic and recreational areas of Monongahela National Forest. Nearby are hiking, Seneca Rocks, Spruce Knob, cave tours, and Canaan Valley Resort State Park.

THE DRIVE

The Dolly Sods lie on the eastern edge of the Allegheny Plateau at an elevation of about 4,050 feet. The high windswept plains and one-sided spruces of the Dolly Sods are a unique piece of the boreal forest in West Virginia, with a climate and plant life similar to parts of northern Canada. The Dolly Sods also provide some of the best views in the state, overlooking ridge after ridge to the east.

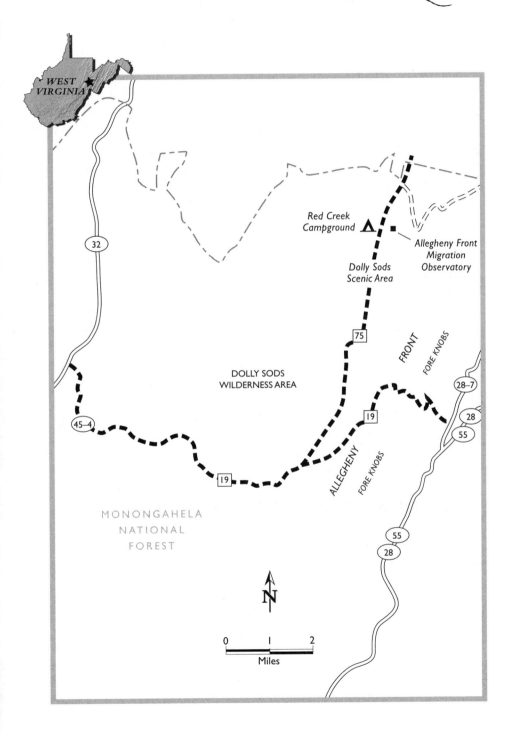

WEST VIRGINIA

Red Creek
Campground

Allegheny Front
Migration
Observatory

Dolly Sods
Scenic Area

32

75

DOLLY SODS
WILDERNESS AREA

FRONT

FORE KNOBS

28–7

28

45–4

19

55

19

ALLEGHENY

FORE KNOBS

MONONGAHELA
NATIONAL
FOREST

55

28

N

0   1   2
Miles

East of the Dolly Sods and some 2,500 feet lower lies the western boundary of the Valley and Ridge province. Connecting the Allegheny Plateau and the Valley and Ridge is a prominent escarpment, the Allegheny Front, which runs northeast-southwest through much of West Virginia.

From the starting point of the drive, at the intersection of WV 28 and FS 19, you traverse about 7 miles of gravel road to climb up the Allegheny Front from an elevation of 1,500 to about 4,050 feet. From there it is another 7 miles on level gravel roads to Bear Rocks, the most scenic part of the Dolly Sods. From Bear Rocks you can continue the drive to Canaan Valley a few miles from Canaan Valley State Park for a total distance of about 30 miles. Or you can take an optional shorter loop that returns to the start of the drive for a total drive of about 25 miles. Whatever way you go from Bear Rocks, it will mostly be on dirt and gravel roads with plenty of downhill stretches. The entire route lies almost entirely within the Monongahela National Forest.

You can make the drive in any vehicle, but make sure the brakes and the cooling system—particularly in warm weather—are in good condition. Do not attempt the drive in winter or at any time in bad weather. Conditions can deteriorate quickly at high elevations. Check with the Forest Service if you have questions about the road or weather. The grades are steep in places, but there are few curves, and the gravel road is wide, with plenty of places to pull over for a respite. If you are not comfortable driving on roads like this, this will be a difficult drive for you. However, the Dolly Sods has unique and outstanding features that can be seen no place else in the continental United States.

The intersection of WV 28 and the beginning of FS 19 is about half a mile north of the intersection of WV 28/55, which is traversed by Drive 13. Look for the Forest Service information board and map; you may want to stop and examine it to help get oriented. Behind the sign are outcrops of nearly vertical beds of sandstone.

ASCENDING THE ALLEGHENY FRONT

Go west (the only way you can) on FS 19. Almost immediately the gravel road starts to climb as you begin the ascent up the Allegheny Front. Maples, dogwood, and other hardwood trees dominate the forest. As you gain altitude occasional views appear through the trees. Partway up is a level, grassy pasture as you pass the ridge at Fore Knobs. Notice that the rock outcrops are no longer vertical but dip more gently to the west. At the top the rocks will lie almost horizontally. Notice also that pines and other conifers begin to mix with the hardwood trees.

White sandstone boulders and stunted spruce trees stand near the edge of the Allegheny Front.

Finally, at the intersection with FS 75, you reach the top of the Allegheny Front, the edge of the Allegheny Plateau, and the edge of the Dolly Sods. Turn right on FS 75, which leads in 7 miles to Bear Rocks. (FS 19 goes straight; you will return here later and continue on FS 19.) Along the way you'll pass several scenic turnouts, trailheads, and the Red Creek Campground.

The area was named for a German settler, John Dahle, a mercenary in the Revolutionary War. He grazed sheep on the otherwise useless dense bluegrass (sod) and farmed nearby. As railroads flourished and West Virginia became more settled in the 1880s, the demand for lumber and wood products led to the widespread cutting of virgin forests throughout the state. The Dolly Sods was no exception, as the huge red spruce and hemlock—some up to 12 feet in diameter—that covered much of the upland succumbed to the saw and ax. The thick humus layer, no longer protected by the forest, quickly dried out and was burned off.

Congress established the Monongahela National Forest in 1920. Despite reforesting efforts by the Forest Service and the Civilian Conservation Corps, the region languished for years, virtually unknown and rarely visited. During

World War II the land was used for target practice as the military hurled thousands of mortar shells onto the barren rocks and heath. Some unexploded mortar shells may still be found in remote areas, despite massive cleanups. These shells are dangerous. If you see one, do not touch it! Report it to the District Ranger in Petersburg.

For 7 miles FS 75 heads north along the top of the 4,000-foot-high plateau. Soon you are driving through nearly treeless heath amid white boulders of sandstone with numerous scenic overlooks. To the east (right), over the Allegheny Front, are spectacular views of the folded rocks of the Valley and Ridge province. On clear days you can see several distinct ridges lined up like giant waves; on especially clear days you may see on the far horizon the Blue Ridge Mountains of Virginia and Shenandoah National Park and Skyline Drive about 30 miles away.

The flat-lying rocks provide a broad, open plateau about 2,500 feet above the valley. The wind is almost constant, sweeping in from the west, with its murmur perpetually in the background. With no significant hills between here and the Rocky Mountains, the wind has more than a thousand miles of fetch to gain strength, and the jet stream often dips down from the stratosphere to howl over the high country. Storms with gale-force winds, dense fog, heavy rain or snow, and a sharply dropping thermometer materialize in a matter of minutes. The harsh climate is more like northern Canada than most of the United States.

The red spruce, stunted and lacking branches on the windward side, give mute testimony to the persistent wind. These one-sided sentinels reliably point east, a compass on the ridge tops. The plant life, surprisingly diverse, abundant, and colorful, closely resembles the boreal forests of northern Canada. Azaleas, mountain laurel, and rhododendron bloom in succession in spring. Summer brings abundant blueberries, huckleberries, and wild cranberries for you to pick and eat. Berries are also favorite foods of West Virginia's state animal, the black bear. As the days cool in autumn, the berry leaves turn ablaze in hues of bright red and orange against the dark green background of the spruce and pines.

The carnivorous insect-eating sundew plant and other plants of the heath can be seen from the boardwalk through the bog on the Northland Loop Trail just before you reach the Red Creek Campground. Stay on the trail to avoid damage to this fragile ecological area. At the campground are twelve primitive campsites, pit toilets, and a picnic area.

The long ridge of the Allegheny Front is a major autumn bird migratory route, and the Allegheny Front Migration Observatory, opposite the camp-

Shaped by the wind, a one-sided spruce struggles for survival.

ground, has become a significant ornithological study area. Mid–September to mid–October is the prime time to see migrating flocks of broad-winged hawks. Thrushes, warblers, and other hawks are common. Don't worry if you are not an experienced birder; when the migration is in full swing there will be plenty of old timers on hand eager to share their knowledge.

Several short trails lead to other scenic areas at the edge of the Allegheny Front. As you look down the Front, notice how quickly the lower slopes are dominated by hardwoods, protected from the harsh winds on the leeward side of the plateau. At Bear Rocks you'll see, well, bare rocks—huge blocks of white sandstone—plus more magnificent views.

The Dolly Sods Scenic Area—approximately 2,000 acres east of FS 75 from FS 19 to Bear Rocks, which you have just driven through—was established in 1970 and is the most visited. A few years later 10,215 acres to the west of FS 75 were designated as the Dolly Sods Wilderness Area. This undeveloped backcountry is traversed by primitive, poorly marked, rough trails intended for experienced hikers and campers. At lower elevations the Dolly Sods Wilderness Area is covered with northern hardwood forests; higher elevations comprise mainly red spruce and heath barrens. Some hikers say the area reminds them of parts of Alaska.

The backcountry also harbors creatures rarely found elsewhere in West Virginia (and rarely seen even here) such as bobcat, Cheat Mountain salamander, and, at the most southern point in its habitat, snowshoe hare. More common are deer, raccoon, woodchuck, skunk, and black bear.

The most popular wilderness trail is the Red Creek Trail, which connects the north and south boundaries. This rocky and wet trail has a few short, steep sections. Because it fords Red Creek twice, it is not passable during high water. Do not attempt hiking here unless you are experienced and equipped for wilderness travel and have first checked with the Forest Service.

THE ANCIENT HISTORY OF THE DOLLY SODS

The Dolly Sods evoke a sense of time and awe in many visitors like no place else in West Virginia. The white sandstone rocks that you see today were deposited more than 300 million years ago during Pennsylvanian time as a beach along the shoreline of the ancient Iapetus Ocean. The swampy land was repeatedly covered by shallow seas and lush marshes. The thick vegetation died and fell into the swampy water, piling up layer after layer to form peat. This was more than 100 million years before dinosaurs, mammals, and flowering plants appeared on Earth.

The beaches and peat were buried under other sediments, compacted, cemented, and finally changed into sandstone and bituminous coal. Some 250 million years ago during ancient continental drift, what is now Africa began to slowly collide into North America from the east, forming the supercontinent known as Pangea. The resulting folding and faulting of the rocks east of the Allegheny Front raised towering mountains 20,000 to 30,000 feet above sea level, similar to the way India today is slowly pushing into Asia to raise the Himalayas.

Later North America and Africa separated, forming the present-day continents with the Atlantic Ocean between them. Millions of years of erosion wore the mountains of Pangea down and flattened the landscape to an almost featureless plain.

About 60 million years ago, eastern North America was uplifted several thousand feet, and streams began to carve the old flat surface into the present hilly topography and stream drainage. In the folded Valley and Ridge province east of Dolly Sods, erosion-resistant sandstones formed the long mountain ridges so prominent today, as the softer limestones and shales were eroded to make the valleys. Thousands of caves, some with scores of miles of passageways, were dissolved out in the soluble limestones in West Virginia. The top of the Allegheny Front was raised higher than the ridgelines to the east, so that its elevation today rises above the tallest peaks to the east; and the Dolly Sods lie at one of the highest points. The Pottsville sandstone here is almost horizontal, giving the plateau-like surface.

A few thousand years ago—the blink of an eye in geologic time—glaciers to the north advanced to within a few hundred miles of West Virginia. The cool climate allowed growth of thick forests of spruce and other northern species; after the glaciers retreated and the climate warmed, the spruce forests continued to flourish on the high windy ridge tops.

Finally came humans, the last chapter in forming the landscape. In the last 130 years we have cut down the huge virgin red spruce and hemlock forest, burned the thick undersoil to allow the unceasing westerly winds to strip the remaining soil down to bare rock, and shot armored shells over the land for military target practice.

Now you can stand on these timeless rocks amid the stunted, one-sided spruce and feel and hear the winds blowing and whistling over the rolling high plateau. As you gaze down on the sinuous ridges and valleys below, consider the changes the land has undergone: ancient beaches and oceans, drifting continents and worn down mountains, erosion and uplift, people and timber. It has all combined to make the scene you see today, and it will be here long after you leave, always awe inspiring, always magnificent.

When you are finally ready to depart, turn around. Retrace the 7 miles along the plateau on FS 75 to the intersection with FS 19. Turn west (right) on FS 19. This will take you to WV 32 about 1.5 miles from Canaan Valley State Park on the southern edge of Drive 9.

Option: If you want to return to the starting point of this drive, do not turn around. Instead, continue north on FS 75 past Bear Rocks and follow FS 75 down the Allegheny Front 4.7 miles to WV 28–7. Turn south (right) on WV 28–7 and drive about 6 miles to the starting point at FS 19, or go another mile to the intersection of WV 28/55.

The main drive heads west, away from the Allegheny Front on FS 75, and borders the Dolly Sods Wilderness Area to the north (right). Hardwood forests cover the land away from the winds on the high plains. After about 1 mile you pass the Dolly Sods Picnic Area. Several trailheads on the left lead into the rugged bogs, cliffs, and plains of the Flat Rock and Roaring Plains. Only experienced hikers should attempt these trails, even though they are better marked and have somewhat less severe weather than those in the wilderness section. They also attract fewer hikers and may appeal to those who crave more solitude.

The drive heads down, down, down, but is not as steep as the drive up the Allegheny Front. As you cross the boundary and leave the Monongahela National Forest, the road becomes paved, a few houses appear, and the route number changes to WV 45–4. A one-lane bridge at Red Creek provides access to a trout stream.

potomac Highlands Loop

SENECA ROCKS AND SMOKE HOLE CANYON

GENERAL DESCRIPTION: A 72-mile loop in the magnificent Potomac Highlands along mountain streams, past towering Seneca Rocks and through unspoiled Smoke Hole Canyon.

SPECIAL ATTRACTIONS: Seneca Rocks, the Allegheny Front, tourist caves, and Smoke Hole Canyon.

LOCATION: East-central West Virginia, between Petersburg and Franklin.

DRIVING ROUTE NUMBERS AND NAME: U.S. 33, 220; WV 28, 55, 2, 2–3, 28–11.

TRAVEL SEASON: Most parts of the drive can be made all year; the section through Smoke Hole Canyon may be closed in winter.

CAMPING: The U.S. Forest Service maintains the eighty-one-unit Seneca Shadows Campground near Seneca Rocks and the fifty-unit Big Bend-Jess Judy Campground in Smoke Hole Canyon, with primitive facilities. Both are open from April through November, with some winter camping permitted. Two private campgrounds near Seneca Rocks are open all year with full facilities.

SERVICES: There are no facilities in Smoke Hole Canyon. Gasoline, food, and lodging are available along other portions of the drive and in Petersburg and Franklin.

NEARBY ATTRACTIONS: Dolly Sods and Spruce Knob.

THE DRIVE

The Potomac Highlands includes the headwaters of the two south branches of the Potomac River adjacent to the imposing Allegheny Front through some of West Virginia's most magnificent scenery. This 72-mile loop heads south along the North Fork past Seneca Rocks, one of West Virginia's best-known landmarks. It then climbs over North Fork Mountain to go north along the South Branch through narrow Smoke Hole Canyon to complete the loop. Along the way are mountain vistas, imposing rock formations, and good fishing, camping, and hiking.

Most of the drive is on paved roads within the Spruce Knob-Seneca Rocks National Recreation Area, which in turn is part of the Monongahela

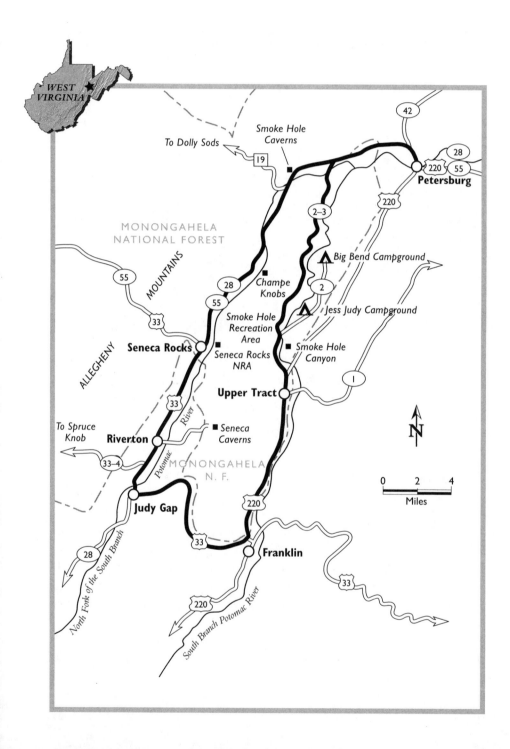

WEST VIRGINIA

42

Smoke Hole Caverns

To Dolly Sods

19

28

220 55

Petersburg

2–3

220

MONONGAHELA NATIONAL FOREST

MOUNTAINS

55

Big Bend Campground

28

Champe Knobs

55

2

33

Smoke Hole Recreation Area

Jess Judy Campground

ALLEGHENY

Seneca Rocks

Seneca Rocks NRA

Smoke Hole Canyon

Upper Tract

1

33

Potomac River

To Spruce Knob

Riverton

Seneca Caverns

33–4

MONONGAHELA N. F.

N

220

0   2   4

Miles

Judy Gap

28

North Fork of the South Branch

33

Franklin

220

33

South Branch Potomac River

National Forest. With many places of interest, the drive will take you all day, but you may want to plan on spending an extra day.

Two additional drives take you through the high country atop the Allegheny Front in the Spruce Knob-Seneca Rocks National Recreation Area. Dolly Sods (see Drive 12) traverses the Arctic-like climate of the high plateau; Spruce Knob (see Drive 14) climbs to the highest point in West Virginia.

From Petersburg drive west on WV 28/55 toward the sweeping vista of the Allegheny Front and Fore Knobs straight ahead. This route follows the North Fork of the South Branch of the Potomac River (known simply as the North Fork) through narrow North Fork Gap into the mountains and the Spruce Knob-Seneca Rocks National Recreation Area in the Monongahela National Forest. Popular with anglers, the entire North Fork, which parallels the drive for the next 30 miles, is usually well stocked with golden trout. Gentle rapids here make it particularly attractive to fly fishermen.

About 6 miles from Petersburg on the left, a bridge leads across the North Fork on WV 28–11. This intersection marks the end of the loop where you will complete the drive later.

Stay on WV 28/55. At 2 miles is the entrance to Smoke Hole Caverns, one of two commercially developed caves along the drive. It features what is called the "world's longest ribbon stalactite." The cave was known to the Indians, who used the entranceway to smoke meat and gave the cave its name. During the Civil War soldiers stored ammunition in the cave; in later years moonshiners used the cold, pure waters of the North Fork to produce their potent beverage, hidden from prying eyes in the recesses of the cave.

Straight ahead and dominating the horizon from left to right is the imposing Allegheny Front, which rises 2,500 feet and more above the highway and includes the highest peaks in West Virginia. The Allegheny Front marks the dividing line between the folded and faulted sedimentary rocks of the Valley and Ridge province to the east (left), which stretch like waves eastward into Virginia, and the flat-lying sediments of the Allegheny Plateau to the west (right). The folding and faulting occurred over several tens of millions of years beginning about 250 million years ago when the ancestral continents of Europe and Asia slowly careened into North America.

Go left (south) on WV 28/55 at the intersection with WV 28–7. Drive 12, which begins about half a mile to the right on WV 28–7 and climbs up the Allegheny Front on dirt roads to the high country of the Dolly Sods. WV 28/55 winds through the deep valley of the North Fork River, rimmed here by North Fork Mountain on the east (left) and the escarpment of Fore Knobs

The North Fork flows past imposing cliffs.

and the Allegheny Front on the west. Soon you pass Champe Knobs, a near-vertical shaft of sandstone jutting several hundred feet into the sky.

APPROACHING SENECA ROCKS

But Champe Knobs is only a precursor to mammoth Seneca Rocks a few miles ahead. Look for it through the twists in the road as you approach the intersection with US 33 and the entrance to the visitor center. An icon of West Virginia, this 900-foot-high behemoth of sandstone was known to Native Americans and was shown on the earliest maps of the state by European settlers.

As one of the most challenging climbs in the east, the bare rock face attracts climbers from around the country. If you want to try your hand and foot at it, two climbing schools will literally show you the ropes even if you are a total beginner. If bare cliffs are not for you, you can still hike the steep West Side Trail 1.3 miles to a safe observation platform just below the ridgeline.

The first recorded climbers scaled the rock in 1938. They thought they were the first, but at the top they were surprised to find carved into the stone "D. B. Sept. 16, 1908." Since then, climbers have developed dozens of routes up the rock face. During World War II, army mountaineer troops came here to train for action in the Alps.

Seneca Rocks also challenges photographers. The west-facing rock is in shadow for most of the day. As the sun illuminates it in the late afternoon, it can shine a brilliant golden or soft yellow with dramatic hues and shadows. Early photographs and postcards show Seneca Rocks as having three humps. In 1987 the center piece, twenty tons of rock known as the Gendarme, suddenly collapsed, leaving Seneca Rocks with its current snaggle-toothed appearance.

Both Champe Knobs and Seneca Rocks were formed in the nearly pure quartz of the Tuscarora sandstone, which has been folded here from its original horizontal position into a near-vertical orientation. The rock formations originally above and below the sandstone—softer shale and limestone—have been eroded away, leaving the imposing cliffs of sandstone.

Other trails lead through the thick woods to scenic overlooks on the ridge behind Seneca Rocks. Ask at the visitor center for information and maps. Exhibits at the visitor center give more details about the geology and plant and bird life, and historic photographs let you compare the rock today with its 1987 precollapse appearance. The visitor center is open daily from late March through Thanksgiving, and on weekends during the rest of the year. Several picnic tables allow you to eat while leisurely examining the rocks.

Seneca Rocks rises 900 feet above the valley.

Next door is the Seneca Shadows Campground, run by the Forest Service, and two private campgrounds are nearby. Worth a visit is Harper's Old Country Store, managed by the same family since 1902 and still maintaining its hundred-year-old ambiance.

From Seneca Rocks continue south (left) on WV 28, now joined by US 33. At Riverton a side trip leads right (east) on WV 9 through a cleft in the Tuscarora sandstone to Germany Valley about 4 miles to Seneca Caverns, the other commercial cave along the drive. The tour through Seneca Caverns is three-quarters of a mile through several large rooms. Because it's not on a main highway, Seneca Caverns has fewer visitors than Smoke Hole Caverns, and some think it is more natural and unspoiled.

Much of the fertile farmland of Germany Valley is underlain by cavernous limestone, and this part of Pendleton County is a frequent destination for those seeking wild or noncommercial caves. Nearby are Hell Hole and Schoolhouse caves, both for experts only, known for their deep pits and sheer drops. Many caving techniques using ropes and mountaineering equipment were first developed in these caves.

Two miles past Riverton on the right at WV 33–4, Briery Gap Road, is the beginning of Drive 14. That drive climbs on gravel roads to Spruce Knob, at 4,863 feet the highest point in West Virginia, and then goes to Spruce Knob Lake, a secluded mountain fishing pond for trout and smallmouth bass.

A mile past Riverton, at Judy Gap, turn south (left) on US 33. WV 28 goes straight. The drive climbs up and over North Fork Mountain, with scenic views of Germany Valley from the top of the ridge. The North Fork Mountain Trail leads north along the ridgeline.

It's a gradual descent to the intersection with US 220 about 13 miles from Judy Gap. Turn north (left) on US 220, which follows the South Branch of the Potomac River, here little more than a stream. (The town of Franklin is about 1 mile ahead on US 220 south.) The countryside is more open and less rugged, with pastureland and numerous farms. The southern boundary of the Monongahela National Forest lies just to the west (left) of the highway.

THROUGH SMOKE HOLE CANYON

About 12 miles from the intersection, past the little town of Upper Tract, turn left on WV 2 at the U.S. Forest Service sign for Smoke Hole Canyon. The South Branch flows through a narrow gap that separates North Fork Mountain from Cave Mountain, with cliffs and slopes 800 to 1,000 feet high on both sides. In several places there is barely room for the road and river.

Past Smoke Hole Canyon are open fields and grazing land.

Swift rapids at Eagle Rock (named not for the bird but for the 1700s set-tler William Eagle), a vertical picturesque pinnacle of sandstone, make the river popular with bass and trout fishermen. Some say that the canyon received its name because of the mist that often fills the valley; others claim that it is named for the smoke that issued from moonshiners' stills. Whatever the case, you soon pass the entrance to Smoke Hole Cave by the side of the road.

About 8 miles from US 220 is an intersection at a little country store. Follow the north (right-hand) branch (WV 2) a few miles along the river past the picnic area to the Jess Judy and Big Bend campgrounds at the end of WV 2. On summer weekends you'll see numerous campers, trailers, and fishermen along this stretch.

Backtrack to the intersection at the store and turn north (right) uphill on WV 2–3. The road leaves the canyon and climbs into the high country where herds of sheep and cattle graze. Until a few years ago, this road was gravel and rough; recent rebuilding and paving have made travel easier. The route num-ber changes to WV 28–3 as you cross the county line.

As you approach North Fork Gap, you'll see talus-covered slopes on the mountains ahead. The drive ends past the bridge of the South Fork at the intersection with WV 28/55, near where you began. Turn right (east) to go to Petersburg; turn left (west) to go to Smoke Hole Caverns and Seneca Rocks.

spruce knob and spruce knob lake

WEST VIRGINIA'S HIGH POINT

GENERAL DESCRIPTION: A 42-mile, curvy drive up the steep Allegheny Front to the observation tower at Spruce Knob, West Virginia's highest point at 4,863 feet elevation. From there, the drive descends to isolated Spruce Knob Lake and then passes along a small fishing creek. Almost the entire drive is on gravel roads.

SPECIAL ATTRACTIONS: Spruce Knob, alpine vegetation, superb views, and Spruce Knob Lake.

LOCATION: East-central West Virginia, west of Franklin.

DRIVING ROUTE NUMBERS AND NAME: WV 29, 33–4; FS 1, 112, 104.

TRAVEL SEASON: Late spring through fall. The road is not maintained in winter.

CAMPING: Spruce Knob Lake has forty-six campsites but no facilities. Nearby is the Gatewood Group Campground. Seneca Shadows at Seneca Rocks has eighty-one campsites with all facilities.

SERVICES: None along the drive. The closest gas is in Riverton.

NEARBY ATTRACTIONS: Seneca Rocks and Seneca Caverns and the Dolly Sods.

THE DRIVE

This 42-mile drive climbs up the 2,500-foot Allegheny Front on gravel roads to the alpine summit of Spruce Knob, the highest point in West Virginia. After a stop at the observation tower, the drive descends to isolated Spruce Knob Lake, then ends about midway between Elkins and Seneca Rocks on US 33/WV 55. The drive has some steep and curvy sections, and almost the entire drive is over gravel roads. It is not suitable for trailers but can be driven

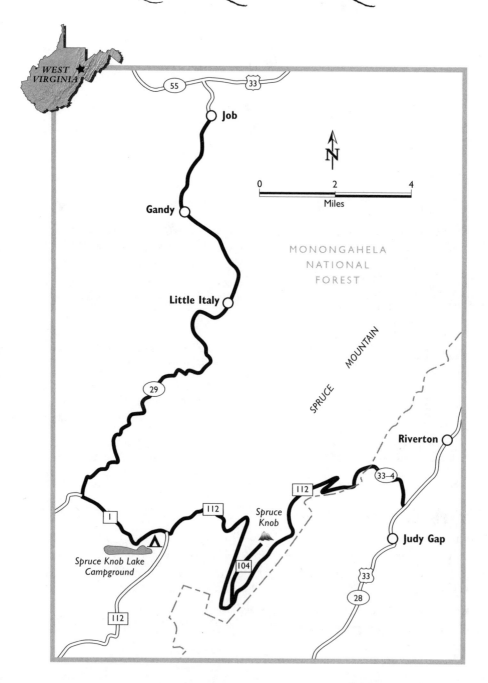

in most passenger vehicles in good condition without four-wheel drive. The drive is not passable in winter, and extreme caution should be used any time of the year. Fog, storms, and snow are possible year-round.

The drive to Spruce Knobs begins at Briery Gap Road, WV 33–4, between Judy Gap and Riverton on US 33/WV 55. Look for the Forest Service sign. The paved but narrow two-lane road leads immediately uphill through predominantly hardwood forests of maple, beech, and oak. Rock outcrops of limestone and sandstone stand nearly vertical, a testimony to the mountain building forces that folded and faulted the rocks millions of years ago.

Bear left at the intersection (follow the signs). The pavement ends as you cross into the Monongahela National Forest and the National Recreation Area, and the route number changes to FS 112. The gravel road goes up, up, up as you continue your ascent of the long ridge of the Allegheny Front, with numerous curves and turns. As you ascend, the hardwood trees become less numerous, giving way to mountain ash, red spruce, and low shrubs that can better withstand the more severe climate at higher elevations.

After 10 miles of uphill work, you reach the top of the ridge about 2,500 feet above the valley at the intersection with FS 104. Turn right on this paved road along an open plateau mostly covered with slabs of sandstone. After passing a picnic area, radio tower, and several scenic views the road ends at 1.9 miles at the Spruce Knob summit parking area. The odds are that it's cold and windy, and the wind is coming from the west.

WEST VIRGINIA'S HIGHEST POINT

From here, a 5-minute walk over the rocky ground leads you to the observation tower. At an elevation of 4,863 feet (some sources show 4,861), Spruce Knob is the highest point in West Virginia. There's no true summit here, just a hump slightly higher than the surrounding terrain, but the view from the two-story tower is magnificent.

To the east and south are waves of ridge after ridge stretching to the horizon. These are the folded rocks of the Valley and Ridge province; on clear days you may see 30 miles to Skyline Drive in Shenandoah National Park in the Blue Ridge Mountains of Virginia.

In other directions the view of the Allegheny Plateau is somewhat less spectacular but no less interesting. The flat-lying rocks of this dissected plateau form a maze of irregular hills and valleys. The closer hills lie within the Monongahela National Forest.

The Allegheny Front extends as an irregular northeast-southwest ridge through much of eastern West Virginia and marks the transition between the

Waves of mountains roll to the horizon.

Valley and Ridge province and the Allegheny Plateau. The apex of this ridge, much of it more than 4,000 feet above sea level, has a climate more like parts of northern Canada than the rest of West Virginia. The Dolly Sods (see Drive 12) lie along this ridge, 25 miles to the northeast.

Adding to the severity of the weather is the constant swoosh of the wind, blowing and blowing and blowing from the west, unfettered in its sweep over the continent. Fog and storms arise quickly, even in summer, and the weather can turn from sunny to snowy in minutes. So strong and so constant is the wind that the western branches of exposed red spruce never develop, and the one-armed trees point eastward as sure as a compass points north.

The rocks here lie flat and horizontal, huge slabs of Tuscarora sandstone undisturbed by the ancient folding and faulting to the east. From the parking area walk the half-mile Whispering Spruce Trail with its outstanding views. Harsh the climate may be, but in the spring, in protected places between the red spruce, you'll see lady slippers, mountain laurel, azaleas, and rhododendron blossom, followed in a few weeks by huckleberries and blueberries for you to pick and enjoy.

The Monongahela National Forest was established in 1920, but it wasn't until 1965 that the Spruce Knob-Seneca Rocks National Recreation Area was created, the first such designation in the country. These recreation areas are developed for public use, and stress access and activity for all users.

All things must eventually end. When you're ready to leave, retrace the drive on FS 104 to the junction with FS 112 and turn right (north). (If you've seen enough, turn left and go back to the starting point.) The pavement ends, and you soon head downhill. Watch for the first hardwood trees as you descend. Several trailheads lead off the road.

SPRUCE KNOB LAKE

Keep left at FS 1. The road to the right leads to the Gatewood Group Campground. After a few more miles you pass the forty-six-site Spruce Knob Lake Campground, and then reach Spruce Knob Lake itself, about 21 miles from the start. The twenty-five-acre lake, surrounded by forests and mountains, is a favorite spot for fishermen seeking bluegills and trout, and includes a wheelchair-accessible fishing pier and a 1-mile boardwalk encircling the lake. To maintain its pristine condition, small electric motors only are permitted on the water, along with canoes and rowboats. Swimming is not permitted.

An angler relaxes on the pier at Spruce Knob Lake.

Back on the road, after a few miles turn right (north) at the stop sign on Rich Mountain Road, WV 29. This nearly level road follows Gandy Creek past fishing camps and picnic areas. A few wilderness campsites are scattered along the road. At mile 32, just as you're getting tired of dirt, particularly if you haven't made any stops, you hit pavement.

The road leaves the national forest. After a few miles you pass the first group of houses, called Little Italy because the first settlers came from, well, you can guess where they came from. The Spring Ridge and Huckleberry Trails lead from the location back into the high country.

From here, it's a few more miles past several small settlements to Job and the intersection with US 33/WV 55. The drive ends here. Turn left (west) to go to Elkins; turn right (east) to go to Seneca Rocks.

Highland Scenic Byway

HIGH PEAKS, BOGS, AND WATERFALLS

GENERAL DESCRIPTION: A 45-mile drive along the Highland Scenic Byway. It first passes through narrow hardwood valleys in Monongahela National Forest, passing by a unique bog and several waterfalls, and climbs into the high peaks of the Allegheny Mountains for unsurpassed views.

SPECIAL ATTRACTIONS: Cranberry Bogs Botanical Area; sweeping vistas; the Falls of Hills Creek; and fishing, hiking, and camping.

LOCATION: Central West Virginia between Richland and Marlinton.

DRIVING ROUTE NUMBERS AND NAME: WV 39/55, 150; 39–S; FS 76, 86, 102.

TRAVEL SEASON: WV 39/55 is open all year; WV 150 is closed from mid-March through December. Spring for the wild-flowers and autumn for the leaf colors are favorite travel times. Travel is usually light.

CAMPING: The US. Forest Service main-tains several campgrounds along the drive, open from mid-March to early December. Backcountry camping is permitted in sev-eral areas.

SERVICES: All services are available at both ends of the drive in Richwood and in nearby Marlinton.

NEARBY ATTRACTIONS: Cass Scenic Railroad and Snowshoe resort (see Drive 17), Greenbrier River Trail, Beartown State Park, Droop Mountain Battlefield State Park, and Watoga State Park (all along Drive 18).

THE DRIVE

For 45 miles the Highland Scenic Byway winds past wooded stream valleys, high country bogs, and mountain vistas on paved, wide roads. The first half of the drive begins in Richwood and follows WV 39/55 east through hard-wood forests with side trips to waterfalls and the unique Cranberry Bog area. This section ends at Cranberry Visitor Center. The remainder of the drive is maintained as a parkway by the U.S. Forest Service. It leads north and east on WV 150 past 4,000-foot peaks of the Allegheny Mountains to end at US 219.

HIGHLAND SCENIC BYWAY

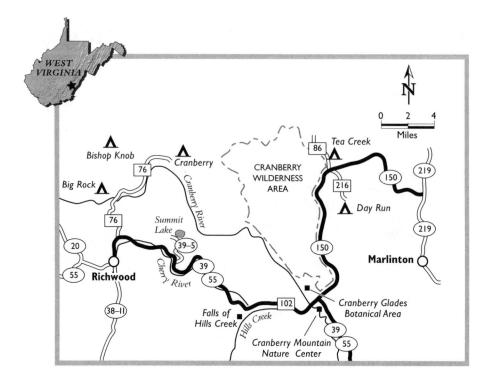

More than 150 miles of hiking trails, from short, wheelchair-accessible boardwalks to strenuous backcountry treks, lead off from the route. Fishing, boating, hunting, and just plain sightseeing are major activities.

The entire drive lies within the Monongahela National Forest and was designated as a National Forest Scenic Byway in 1989. It is one of three West Virginia highways that have been designated as a National Scenic Byway by the U.S. Secretary of Transportation; the others are the George Washington Heritage Trail (see Drives 6 and 7) and the Coal Heritage Trail (see Drive 23).

The town of Richwood on the Cherry River lies at the western end of the drive, surrounded by the Monongahela National Forest. The town, originally named Cherry Tree Bottoms, was a lumber and mill town in the early 1900s. Much of that wood was processed locally into clothespins in what was then the world's first and largest clothespin factory.

Timber is still important today, but the town is better known as a gateway to recreational activities in the Monongahela National Forest. The town is the southern trailhead for the Cranberry Tri-River Trail, which follows a former railroad bed past woods, over trestles, and through tunnels for 14.5 miles. The trail gets its name because it meanders along portions of the Cherry, Gauley, and Cranberry Rivers.

Each April since 1937 Richwood has been host to the annual Feast of the Ramson. This festival honors the wild leek or ramp, *Allium tricoccum,* which grows abundantly in springtime in the surrounding hills and woods. Its bulbous, strong, and aromatic root is savored by many, despite the strong and lingering odor. You can fry ramps to eat with potatoes, ham, or eggs, stuff them, serve them in soups or salads—but the true connoisseurs eat them raw.

From Richwood drive east on WV 39/55. Just outside of town a side road, FS 76, winds north (left) along the Cranberry River, a prime trout fishing stream. FS 76 leads after 5 miles to a picnic area and the Big Rock Campground with five sites, and after another 6 miles to the Cranberry Campground with thirty sites. These fishing sites are usually less crowded than other sites closer to the main highway.

The drive enters the designated Scenic Byway at the Gauley Ranger Station and then passes through thick forests of beech, maple, oak, poplar, hemlock, and red spruce. About 8 miles from Richwood, just past the North Bend Picnic Area, another side road, WV 39–5, leads after 2 miles to Summit Lake and the Summit Lake Campground with thirty-three sites. The forty-two-acre lake, cherished by trout and bass fishermen, has a boat ramp and a wheelchair-accessible fishing pier. Several trails, ranging from an easy 1.5-mile footpath with views of the lake and surrounding forest and hills to strenuous hikes into the national forest, begin here.

THE FALLS OF HILLS CREEK

Back on the main drive, about 16 miles from Richwood is the turnoff for the Falls of Hills Creek Scenic Area, where three waterfalls plummet over cliffs of shale and sandstone. The first waterfall, 25 feet high, is reached on a paved, wheelchair-accessible trail that has several steep grades. An unpaved and steeper trail continues downhill three-quarters of a mile to two more falls that are 45 and 63 feet high. Observation platforms at each falls give you unobstructed views of the falling and rushing water. The 63-foot fall is the second largest in the state.

The drive continues over a pass into a high bowl-like valley. Turn left (north) on FS 102 for 1.5 miles to the parking area and boardwalk in the 750-acre Cranberry Glades Botanical Area, a national natural landmark. (Before visiting the botanical area, you may want to proceed to the Cranberry Mountain Nature Center, 1 mile ahead on WV 39/55, for information and

Highland Scenic Byway

maps.) At an elevation of 3,400 feet, the tundra-like bowl preserves several bogs that contain a relic population of plants more commonly found in northern Canada. These plants, including several varieties of orchids, the carnivorous sundew, monkshood, jack-in-the-pulpit, and skunk cabbage, flourished over large areas of West Virginia several thousand years ago when glaciers lay to the north. Now they are found in only a few high mountain areas of the state.

BOGS IN THE WILDERNESS

The bogs lie on the edge of 26,000 acres of unspoiled backcountry called the Cranberry Wilderness Area. Locally called "glades," the bogs consist of spongy peat (partially decayed plant material) covered by sphagnum moss. A wheelchair-accessible boardwalk leads for half a mile through the bogs and the surrounding bog forest of red spruce, hemlock, and yellow birch. Stay on the boardwalk to protect this fragile area.

The boardwalk is open 24 hours a day. Early morning is the best time to see birds, including the northern water thrush (here at the southern limit of its range). Forest Service rangers conduct bog nature walks on weekend afternoons during the summer months. Check at the Cranberry Mountain Nature Center (next stop) for details.

You can drive another mile north on FS 102 to a barrier at the edge of the wilderness area. The road continues as a hiking trail with access to an extensive trail network. A favorite is the Cow Pasture Trail, a 6-mile loop through the wilderness, with views of numerous beaver ponds and alder thickets.

Turn around, return to WV 39/55, and turn left (east). The Cranberry Mountain Nature Center is about 1 mile down the road, at the junction of WV 39/55 and WV 150, about 23 miles from Richwood. The center, open from April through November, provides displays, maps, hiking and camping information, and interpretive programs about the area. Ask here about conducted tours of the Cranberry Glades Botanical Area and special programs. There are usually temporary exhibits of small animals such as turtles, snakes, and insects, which are returned to the wild after a week or two.

From the nature center, turn left (north) on WV 150. This is the beginning of the spectacular highland section of the drive, a 22-mile parkway that is the highest major road in West Virginia. The U.S. Forest Service manages the road through the Allegheny Mountains for its scenic and recreational use.

Commercial vehicles are banned at all times. The road is not maintained in winter and is usually closed by snow from early December through March.

Visitors head into the bog at the Cranberry Wilderness Area.

Watery "glades" support thick growths of aquatic plants.

The 45-mile-an-hour speed limit gives you plenty of time to enjoy the scenery. Numerous overlooks give you scenic views in all directions; all of them are provided with wheelchair-accessible picnic shelters and restrooms. This wide, two-lane paved highway, in contrast to many other West Virginia mountain roads, has a minimum of curves and steep grades and is negotiable by all but the longest RVs.

ON TOP OF THE BYWAY

High it is: More than 60 percent of the parkway is above 4,000 feet, and a whopping 88 percent is above 3,500 feet. It traverses the eastern boundary of the Cranberry Wilderness Area, with more than 70 miles of hiking trails leading off into the backcountry.

As the road climbs to follow the crest of Black Mountain, the hardwood forests give way to red spruce and stunted scrub forest. Ridge tops are capped by a line of dark green spruce needles; the lighter green leaves of deciduous trees predominate at lower elevations. Several overlooks provide views into the Cranberry Glades and the Williams River Valley.

The road then dips down into the 3,000-foot-high river valley to cross the Williams River and FS 86 about 14 miles from the nature center. The Williams River is kept stocked with brown, rainbow, and brook trout; as you may guess, this makes it a popular fishing stream. FS 86 leads north about 1 mile to the Tea Creek Campground, with fourteen sites, and south 4 miles to the Day Run Campground, also with fourteen sites.

After a gradual climb up Tea Creek Mountain, the road follows the high skyline for the rest of the drive, with almost constant views. At the Williams River Overlook, elevation 4,000 feet, you can look back at the river valley and look ahead to see the road as its sweeps over ridge after ridge. At other overlooks you may be able to see the extensive developments along the ridgeline to the east at the Snowshoe resort and ski area.

The drive gradually descends to end at US 219 at an elevation of 3,525 feet, 7 miles north of Marlinton.

16

Railroad Loop and the National Radio Astronomy Observatory

CASS AND DURBIN RAILROADS

GENERAL DESCRIPTION: A 30-mile drive through woods and fields of the Monongahela National Forest past two scenic railroads and the National Radio Astronomy Observatory. An optional return loop on a mountain road adds 16 miles.

SPECIAL ATTRACTIONS: Snowshoe Mountain Resort, Cass Scenic Railroad State Park, the National Radio Astronomy Observatory, and Durbin Route Scenic Railroad.

LOCATION: East-central West Virginia, about 35 miles south of Elkins.

DRIVING ROUTE NUMBERS AND NAME: US 219, 250, WV 1, 28/92, 66.

TRAVEL SEASON: Late spring through October. The scenic railroads operate daily from Memorial Day to Labor Day, with weekend trips through the middle of October; tours of the National Radio

Astronomy Observatory follow a similar calendar.

CAMPING: The Island Campground, in the Monongahela National Forest east of Durbin on WV 28, has five primitive campsites and is the only public campground near the drive. Near Cass and north of Arborvale are several private campgrounds with all facilities.

SERVICES: All services are available at Snowshoe. Reservations are recommended year-round and are a necessity during the ski season. Gasoline and food are available in all towns along the drive, with limited overnight facilities along the route.

NEARBY ATTRACTIONS: Gaudineer Scenic Area, Greenbrier River Trail, Elk River Touring Center, and Cheat Mountain Salamander Scenic Railroad.

16 RAILROAD LOOP AND THE NATIONAL RADIO ASTRONOMY OBSERVATORY

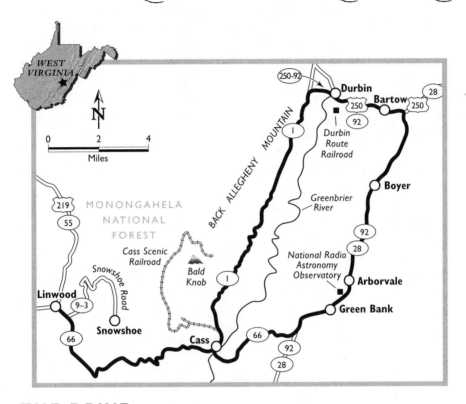

THE DRIVE

Toot! Toot! All aboard! Chug-chug! Chug-chug! West Virginia has more than a dozen scenic train trips, and this drive takes you by two of them.

One is the long-established Cass Scenic Railroad State Park. This train, powered by a restored logging steam locomotive, huffs, puffs, and climbs by switchbacks to the top of Bald Knob, the third-highest peak in the state. The other, the lesser-known and privately owned Durbin Route, chugs along the isolated banks of the upper Greenbrier River pulled by a small diesel. Both trains offer a variety of trips.

The drive also takes you to the mountaintop resort town of Snowshoe, with its hodgepodge of ski lifts, condos, shops, and magnificent views. And if you'd rather ponder the far reaches of the universe, stop in Green Bank at the

National Radio Astronomy Observatory (NRAO) where, in an isolated valley, domes and radio telescopes reach out for signals from outer space.

The drive begins at the intersection of WV 66 and US 219/WV 55 about 2 miles from the entrance to Snowshoe and 12 miles west of Cass. After visiting Snowshoe, the drive continues on WV 66 to Cass and the scenic railroad. From Cass, continue east WV 66 to the intersection with WV 28/92. Follow WV 28/92 for about 12 miles, stopping to visit the NRAO, to the intersection with US 250 and WV 92. From there it is 4 miles to the scenic railroad at Durbin and the end of the drive, for a total of about 30 miles. Most of the drive is through rolling country with gentle hills, past forests, fields, and small towns; all of it is over two-lane, paved primary highways, suitable for all vehicles. The entire drive lies within the boundaries of the Monongahela National Forest, but much of the land along the route is still privately owned.

You can make this a loop drive by returning from Durbin to Cass on WV 1—better known as Back Mountain Road—a paved but narrow, steep, and winding road about halfway up Back Allegheny Mountain with numerous scenic vistas. This 16-mile stretch is not recommended for trailers or for drivers who do not like mountain driving, and it will take you longer than retracing the drive along the state highways.

Begin the drive by going south on WV 66 where it intersects with US 219/WV 55. After a few miles you pass the entrance on the left to Snowshoe Mountain Resort, 2 miles uphill from WV 66. It's worth a trip, even if you do nothing else but look around to see what developers can do to a mountaintop.

With more than fifty ski slopes and a dozen lifts, Snowshoe has been known for years as a major destination for winter sports enthusiasts. To keep its ridge-hugging lodges, shops, and restaurants busy and profitable during the rest of the year, the resort has added a golf course, more than a hundred miles of mountain biking trails, tennis, and hiking, plus cultural events from symphonies to poetry reading.

FROM SNOWSHOE TO CASS

When you leave Snowshoe, return to WV 66 and turn east (left). It's about a 10-mile, mostly downhill drive through woods and fields to Cass and the Cass Scenic Railroad State Park. The drive into town passes through the historical district, where numerous buildings have been restored to look as they did around 1911 when Cass was a major timber center. Beyond that are the huge general store, the railroad tracks (usually with trains belching steam), and the depot where you purchase tickets.

The station at Cass Scenic Railroad.

Railroads have been a vital part of West Virginia's transportation and economy for more than a hundred years. By 1900, when coal and lumber were West Virginia's major industries, a 3,000-mile network of railroad tracks spider-webbed the state. The coal and lumber were hauled by horse and mule or narrow gauge trains from mines and forests deep in the remote mountains to sidings by the main lines. There they were loaded onto long trains headed by powerful steam-driven and diesel locomotives that pulled the hundreds of coal- and timber-laden cars to market.

After World War II both the coal and lumber industries went into prolonged declines. The coal-powered steam engines were replaced by modern diesels, but rail transportation decreased as the public took to the highways in their new postwar cars. As the interstate system and other new roads were built and old ones improved, much of the hauling previously done by rail was taken over by trucks. Small coal mines and lumbering operations were particularly hard hit, and hundreds closed down.

For several decades all but the main lines of the railroads were abandoned and virtually forgotten. As they languished, the rights-of-way were returned to near wilderness again as the forest slowly took over. In the 1990s the abandoned rail rights-of-way began to be recognized as national treasures and were revered for their scenic beauty and potential recreational activities.

Today almost every state has seen the rebirth of former railroads for hiking, biking, and equestrian trails and elongated parks. In West Virginia, the Greenbrier River Trail, which has its northern trailhead in Cass, and the North Bend Rail Trail each provide more than 70 miles of trails over old rail beds; throughout the state several hundred miles of trails follow former railroads.

The trains themselves have made a comeback as scenic railroads—almost a dozen in West Virginia—prime tourist attractions that give their riders fast and easy access to many of the scenic and remote areas of the state. The two best known are the Cass Scenic Railroad and the Potomac Eagle in Romney (Drive 5).

At Cass, as at other logging centers, trees were cut down on the steep mountainsides, loaded onto logging trains, and hauled to the mill. Trains had to negotiate steep grades and hairpin curves, often over temporary tracks. This required locomotives built for power and maneuverability, with speed a distant secondary consideration.

Riders return to the train after a picnic stop on the way to Bald Knob.

Today's trains carry not timber but tourists in comfortable, refurbished, open logging flatbeds. Steam locomotives, such as the 160-ton Shay, blow their shrill whistles and then huff, puff, and chug as they haul their load of riders up the steep mountainsides. Several narrated train trips are offered. The longest takes four and one-half hours and climbs to the summit of Bald Knob, the second highest point in the state at 4,842 feet, with views on clear days to the Blue Ridge Mountains of Virginia.

Trains run daily from Memorial Day through Labor Day and on weekends until late October, with special dinner trains and fall foliage trips. Purchase tickets at the depot by the tracks. While waiting for your train, you can visit the historical district, the bustling Cass Country Store, the Wildlife Museum, and the combined Historical Museum and Cass Showcase, filled with railroad and logging memorabilia.

SPOTLIGHT ON OUTER SPACE

Back in the car, continue east on WV 66 through the thick hardwood woodlands of the Monongahela National Forest. As you come out of the woods into open fields, look to your left. About 1 mile away, on the grounds of the National Radio Astronomy Observatory, you'll see the giant dish of the world's largest radio telescope probing into the sky.

Turn left (north) at the stop sign at the junction with WV 28/92. More satellite dishes and domes appear, leading in about 2 miles to the entrance on the left to the NRAO in the town of Green Bank. This facility is one of the few observatories that study and analyze radio waves from space. Most telescopes look at the visible portion of the spectrum, the light waves that we see. The telescopes here study radio waves with wavelengths that range from a few millimeters to many meters. These waves emanate from the universe around us, from galaxies millions of light years away, and from celestial objects such as pulsars and quasars.

The NRAO, a facility of the National Science Foundation, was created in 1958 and sited in this remote valley to protect the sensitive receivers from human-made radio interference. The telescope you saw from the road began operation in late 1999 and was christened the Robert C. Byrd Green Bank Telescope in honor of West Virginia's prominent U. S. senator. The GBT, as it is known, stands more than 480 feet high, with the reflector measuring more than 300 by 330 feet. Its surface is adjustable to correct for minute changes from the temperature or the weight of the telescope. Scientists using it study the structure and chemistry of space and seek answers to what were formerly philosophical questions such as the nature of time and the origin of space time.

Radio telescopes are poised to study radio waves at the NRAO in Green Bank.

Some other telescopes are used in research here, including the world's largest equatorial mounted radio telescope, 140 feet high. Students gain experience on a 40-inch scope. Visitors are free to wander through most of the grounds, but only on foot: Motorized vehicles, except for some specially outfitted ones, would interfere with the radio signals. Free guided tours are conducted daily in summer and on weekends in spring and fall. Special programs are held throughout the year; check the Web site listed in the Appendix for the latest offerings.

An airstrip helps more than 250 scientists from around the world use the research facilities here each year. Some say that the town of Green Bank has the highest proportion of Ph.D.s per capita in the country. If you are one of the thousands who use a home computer to help search for intelligence beyond the Earth, you probably already know that the Search for Extraterrestrial Intelligence (SETI) project (originally project OZMA) was launched here in 1960.

When you leave the NRAO, turn left and continue north on WV 28/92. The drive continues along the level valley with no major hills, paralleling Back Allegheny Mountain to the left. At the junction with US 250, turn north (left) on US 250/WV 92 and drive about 4 miles to Durbin and the station for the Durbin Route Scenic Railroad.

THE DURBIN ROUTE RAILROAD

A smaller operation than Cass, the Durbin Route is one of three scenic railroads owned and operated by the Durbin and Greenbrier Railroad. The Durbin Route winds along the upper unspoiled reaches of the Greenbrier River. Riders have their choice of riding in an old wooden caboose or in an open observation car, both pulled by a small diesel engine, for a one-and-a-half-hour, 10-mile round trip. Wildlife is often abundant along this isolated river, including herons, waterfowl, and deer.

The railroad runs several trips daily during the warmer months and on weekends in spring and fall. Across the street from the station is the Rail and Trail Store. The Durbin and Greenbrier Railroad operates two other scenic train trips: the Cheat Mountain Salamander, about 10 miles north of Durbin, and the New Tygart Flyer, which runs between Belington and Elkins.

The main drive ends in Durbin. An optional return loop to Cass runs along the slope of Back Allegheny Mountain about halfway up the mountainside. This route is not recommended for trailers, large RVs, or drivers who do not like mountain driving. This 16-mile stretch is shorter than backtracking the way you came but will take longer.

You can ride in the caboose or the open gondola on the Durbin Route.

To take this return loop, from Cass go north on US 250/WV 92, which climbs up Back Allegheny Mountain. After about 1 mile turn left (south) on WV 1, Back Mountain Road, and follow the road back to Cass. The road is paved, but it is barely two lanes wide and narrow, hilly, and very curvy. Go slow, because most curves do not have warning signs as you approach them. Most of the land along the route is used for grazing, with some scenic vistas and woods, but with few houses and little flat ground. The optional loop ends in Cass by the railroad depot.

17

New River Gorge and Bridge

INTO AND OUT OF THE NEW RIVER GORGE

GENERAL DESCRIPTION: Twisting, curving, and descending 1,000 feet from the canyon rim to river level, this 16-mile drive follows the old highway into the gorge of the New River, crosses the river, climbs up the other side of the gorge, and drives across the modern New River Gorge Bridge 876 feet above the river. It ends at the Canyon Rim Visitor Center of the New River Gorge National River. The drive is not suitable for mobile homes or large vehicles.

SPECIAL ATTRACTIONS: Challenging driving and spectacular views from above and below of the gorge and bridge.

LOCATION: South-central West Virginia near Fayetteville.

DRIVING ROUTE NUMBERS AND NAME: US 19; WV 82.

TRAVEL SEASON: All year, but snow may temporarily close the drive in winter.

Travel is heaviest when fall colors are at their peak in late September and October, and reaches a crescendo on Bridge Day weekend in late October.

CAMPING: Public camping at nearby Babcock State Park, and more distantly at Pipestem and Bluestone State Parks. More than half a dozen private campgrounds can be found in the Fayetteville area.

SERVICES: All services are available in Fayetteville at the end of the drive, but no services are available along the drive itself.

NEARBY ATTRACTIONS: Thurmond Depot (Drive 19), Grandview Visitor Center, Sandstone Falls, all part of the New River Gorge National River. Also nearby is the African-American Heritage Family Tree Museum in Ansted, the Beckley Exhibition Coal Mine, and Tamarack, West Virginia's arts and crafts exhibition and outlet center.

THE DRIVE

Held in awe by white-water enthusiasts, the New River, now preserved as the New River Gorge National River, surges through a 1,000-foot-deep canyon in southern West Virginia. The New River and the nearby Gauley are known for their Class III to Class V+ rapids, the best and wildest white water in the country east of the Rockies.

The New River Gorge Bridge carries US 19 traffic almost 900 feet above the New River.

Pretty it may be, but for many years the 14-mile-long New River Gorge presented a formidable barrier to travel. Crossing this canyon entailed a long drive down winding mountain roads and an equally arduous drive up the other side. This ended in October 1977, when the 3,030-foot-long New River Gorge Bridge opened. The span reduced the gorge crossing to about a minute, as motorists whisk along US 19, 876 feet above the river.

This drive follows the old road into the New River Gorge on WV 82, a paved, but narrow, very steep, and curvy road. It then crosses the New River and climbs up the other side on an uphill and equally curvaceous road. At the top, near Fayetteville, the drive follows US 19 across the New River Gorge Bridge to the National Park Service's Canyon Rim Visitor Center. The drive is only 16 miles long, but the curves and grades will make it seem a lot longer.

This drive is not suitable for mobile homes, towed vehicles, and other large vehicles. If you are not comfortable driving on mountain roads, do not take this drive. Although the entire route is on paved roads, WV 82 is a twisting roller coaster ride, even by West Virginia standards. Whether or not you take the complete drive, you can still enjoy the drive over the bridge on US 19 and the views, wildlife, exhibits, and activities at the Canyon Rim Visitor Center.

17 NEW RIVER GORGE AND BRIDGE

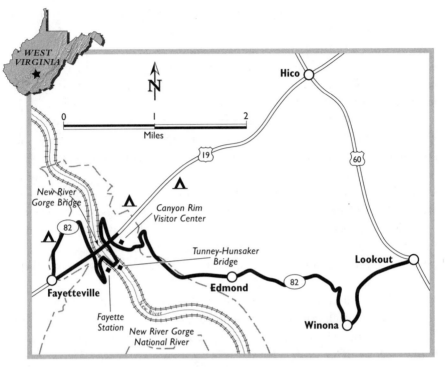

The drive starts at the town of Lookout, near mile 57 on US 60 at the intersection of US 60 and WV 82. Go west on WV 82, which is narrow and curvy but paved and well maintained.

The road soon heads downhill. At first the grades are easy, a warm-up for what lies ahead, and there is enough flat ground for some farming. Turn right at the stop sign in Winona, still following WV 82.

At the tiny post office in Edmond, bear left. One of the smallest in the state, this post office has about enough room for the postmistress and two patrons. Edmond lies almost on the edge of the gorge, and the grades steepen as you descend below the level of the canyon lip.

DESCENDING INTO THE GORGE

After you cross the boundary into the national river area, the road goes down, down, down, with numerous sharp curves. WV 82 goes left at the fork, at a small parking area for hikers and rock climbers. Beyond the fork, the road becomes one-way as it hugs the sheer cliff. (This fork is your last chance to bail out before the steepest and curviest part of the drive. If more curves and more grades are not to your liking, go right on the unnumbered road, which will eventually lead you to US 19 near the Canyon Rim Visitor Center.)

You'll encounter constant hairpin curves, switchbacks, and steep downgrades from here—too many to show them all on the map—with occasional pull-offs for hikers, sightseers, and rock climbers. If it seems like a difficult trip, remember that before 1973 this was the only way to cross the river. You'll have numerous views of the river and the span, supports, and undersides of the New River Gorge Bridge as the drive crosses and recrosses below it.

The rocks and cliffs of the gorge are sedimentary rocks, deposited during the Mississippian and Pennsylvanian periods, 320 to 330 million years old. The vertical cliffs are well-cemented sandstone and conglomerate; the gentler slopes are made up of shale, siltstone, and thin beds of limestone. Rhododendron and mountain laurel grow in profusion on all but the sheerest of cliffs, and hardwood trees cover any remaining snippets of level ground.

Most of the rocks were deposited as sediments in shallow water or swamps from the erosion and redeposition of previously existing rocks; the most probable source area was a highland to the southeast about where the Blue Ridge Mountains are located today.

The sheer cliffs, known to geologists as the Nuttall sandstone and to rock climbers as The Wall, extend for many miles along the gorge with few breaks. About 1,400 rock climbing routes have been established; many are described in the FalconGuides, *Rock Climbing Virginia, West Virginia, and Maryland* and *New River Rock,* published by The Globe Pequot Press. Most are for expert or advanced climbers and rated 5.9 or higher.

Numerous coal seams are dispersed throughout the section, some of which are still mined nearby. The coal beds formed in swamps and shallows from dead plants and trees whose fossil remains can often be seen in the coal. The most notable coal deposit is the 6-foot-thick Sewell seam, once widely known as the "Famous New River Smokeless Coal." Miners were especially fond of this coal seam, both for its profitable high-grade coal and for its tall underground passages that let them walk upright. The ghost town of Sewell, once a thriving mining town, lies along the bottom of the gorge a few miles to the south.

When the Appalachian Mountains were uplifted and folded beginning 225 million years ago, the rocks in the New River area were tilted to the northwest at about 60 feet per mile. By adding up and totaling the thickness of all rock layers in the area, a maximum thickness of some 4,000 feet is obtained. Because the maximum depth of the gorge is about 1,600 feet, only a fraction of the complete section can be seen at any one spot.

After a final curve and downgrade, the road reaches Fayette Station, which is little more than a narrow ledge of level land at the bottom of the V-shaped valley. The road, the railroad, and the river share the cramped space, with steep cliffs rising up on both sides. Like most of the former coal mining towns along the New River, little remains of the town of Fayette Station. The New River, about a hundred yards wide here, looks fairly benign. But the sound of the river is always in the background—a minor gurgle in low water; a thundering bellow when the river runs full, giving a hint of its bone-rattling rapids farther upstream.

Watch for trains as you cross the tracks; this is the main line of the CSX and still in active use. Railroads were vital to the development of the coal industry and the economy of West Virginia. Laying tracks along river valleys such as the New was a challenge, but it was cheaper and faster than blasting the tunnels and constructing the bridges and trestles that were needed to build rail systems in other parts of the state. Diesel engines have replaced the coal-driven locomotives, but freight trains, some with multiple engines hauling several hundred cars filled with coal, still snake their way through the canyon. Amtrak passenger trains, most equipped with scenic observation cars, provide sightseers with a closeup view of the canyon.

Several parking spots give you a chance to pull over and admire the river and canyon at your leisure. Many raft and boat trips conclude here. The take-out areas give you a closeup look at the water and allow fishermen to try their luck hooking the numerous smallmouth bass and walleyes.

How old is the New River? Its deep gorge and the fact that it apparently flows completely across the Appalachian Mountains from east to west have often led to the claim that it is the second oldest river in the world after the Nile. But there is no accurate way of dating a river. The New must be younger than the enclosing rocks (320 million years old). It must also be younger than both the beginning of the Appalachian Mountain building (225 million years) and the last remnant of the Appalachian uplift (65 million years ago).

The New also doesn't flow completely across the Appalachians, and it is one of at least eight rivers that rise in the Appalachians and also flow west. Studies of the erosion rates of major rivers of the United States yield a figure of about 1 foot of erosion every 6,000 years; this yields an age of about 10 million years to erode 1,600 feet of the gorge. Erosion studies of the Grand Canyon of Arizona give it an estimated age of between 5 and 10 million years; the New at its maximum depth is about one-third as deep as the Grand Canyon, so these figures give it an age of between two and three million years.

AT THE BOTTOM OF THE GORGE

Eventually you reach the narrow bridge across the New River. The present bridge, known as the Tunney-Hunsaker Bridge, was built in 1997 in hopes that a modern structure would better withstand the yearly floods that had wiped out a long line of predecessors. A parking area gives you a chance to walk across the bridge. The last major rapids of the New River Gorge lie several hundred feet upstream to the left (southeast), and if your timing is good you may see rafts or kayaks (and hear the shouts of the rafters) as they traverse this final stretch of white water and then pass under the bridge.

After crossing the bridge, the drive turns right. In the distance are the spans of the New River Gorge Bridge. What goes down must eventually go up, and soon you begin the ascent out of the gorge. This side is every bit as curvy and hilly as the descent, crossing under the New River Gorge Bridge several times. After leaving the gorge, you pass numerous rafting and rock climbing outfitters.

WV 82 ends at the stop sign at the intersection with US 19 on the eastern edge of Fayetteville. Only 14 miles from the start in Lookout, it probably seems much longer. Turn right (west) on US 19 to visit downtown Fayetteville; turn left (east) to cross the New River Gorge Bridge and go to the Canyon Rim Visitor Center.

Fayetteville's main industry today is catering to the needs of the thousands of kayakers, rafters, rock climbers, hikers, and other outdoor-loving visitors who come to the area. Some two dozen white-water rafting companies are located in town or nearby. (See the Appendix for numbers for the West Virginia Division of Tourism and the Fayetteville Visitors Center. There are too many rafting companies to list them individually.) Fayetteville's homey atmosphere is enhanced by a partially restored historic area and numerous restaurants that help satiate the gargantuan appetites brought on by an energetic day on the river.

ACROSS THE NEW RIVER GORGE BRIDGE

After gazing at the underside of the New River Gorge Bridge, you should now be ready to drive over it. The bridge is about 1 mile east of Fayetteville on US 19. Try to drive over it slowly, looking down almost 900 feet at where you've been. If you look to the right you may be able to spy the tiny bridge at Fayette Station and other views of the roads you've just traversed.

If you want to *walk* over the bridge, come back on Bridge Day, the third Saturday in October, the one day of the year when the bridge is open to foot traffic. You will have to share the road with more than a quarter of a million

A flotilla of rafts passes below the New River Gorge Bridge.

other visitors who come to marvel at the view; watch the rappellers and parachutists drop over the side; take a guided walk; or just enjoy the food, music, and souvenirs supplied by hundreds of vendors. This gala affair, sponsored by the Fayette County Chamber of Commerce, has become West Virginia's largest festival. Parking for this event is spread out for several miles in both directions along US 19.

From the end of the bridge, it's another minute to reach the Canyon Rim Visitor Center and the end of the drive. This visitor center, the largest in the park, contains museum and slide exhibits on the history and natural features of the area. A wheelchair-accessible walkway leads to an observation deck at the edge of the gorge for views of the bridge and gorge; another boardwalk descends 100 feet into the gorge. Rangers are available for additional information and for conducted talks and tours. A variety of trails start here, ranging from an easy loop along the rim of the trail to an arduous round-trip trek to the bottom of the gorge and back.

Greenbrier River Valley

LEWISBURG TO MARLINTON

GENERAL DESCRIPTION: This nearly level 44-mile drive follows the verdant valley of the gentle Greenbrier River, known for its outstanding hiking, boating, and fishing. It passes caves, Civil War battle sites, intriguing rock formations, and the birthplace and museum of author Pearl S. Buck, winner of both the Nobel and Pulitzer prizes.

SPECIAL ATTRACTIONS: Lost World Caverns, the Greenbrier River Trail, Beartown State Park, Pearl S. Buck Museum, and Droop Mountain Battlefield and Watoga State Park.

LOCATION: Southeast West Virginia, off I-64, exit 169, near White Sulphur Springs 14 miles from the Virginia border.

DRIVING ROUTE NUMBERS AND NAME: US 219; WV 39/55.

TRAVEL SEASON: All year. Spring and fall are the most popular and most colorful travel times.

CAMPING: Watoga State Park has two campgrounds with eighty-eight sites, most with hookups. The Greenbrier River Trail has several primitive campsites. Marlinton has a small municipal campground. There are private campgrounds at Lewisburg and Marlinton.

SERVICES: All services in Lewisburg and Marlinton. Gas and food are available in Hillsboro and most of the small towns along the drive.

NEARBY ATTRACTIONS: Organ Cave, Watoga State Park, Cranberry Glades Botanical Area, Highland Scenic Drive, Cass Scenic Railroad, Greenbrier State Forest, and The Greenbrier, a resort in White Sulphur Springs.

THE DRIVE

At the beginning of the twentieth century, the Greenbrier River Valley was a thriving lumbering area, as trains loaded with timber for the growing cities on the eastern seaboard chugged their way through the valley. Today the trains are gone, and the formerly bare hills are again covered with hardwood forests. The former railroad is also gone; in its place is the Greenbrier River Trail State Park, a shoestring hiking and biking trial that winds along the river for 80 miles.

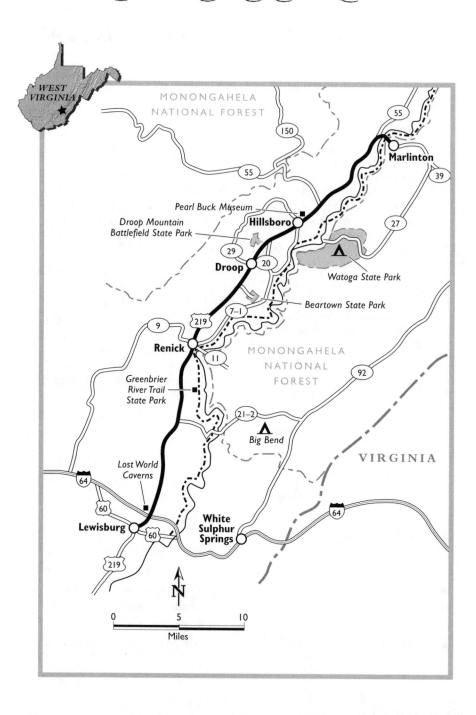

Parallel to the Greenbrier River, US 219 also winds northward. This drive follows US 219 and the Greenbrier Valley for 44 miles from Lewisburg to Marlinton. The valley, wide at Lewisburg, becomes narrower and more wooded as you head north. Both sides of the drive are bordered by the Monongahela National Forest.

In addition to the Greenbrier River Trail, other outstanding natural and historical places lie along the drive, which gives you a variety of choices to plan your visit. Notable are the scenic commercial Lost River Caverns, the rocks and canyons of Beartown, the Civil War battlefield at Droop Mountain, Pearl S. Buck's birthplace and museum, the rugged hills and woods of Watoga State Park, and the historic town of Marlinton. Side trips to some of these places will add another 10 miles or so to the mileage. You can traverse the entire route in little over an hour, but if you want to hike, walk, fish, swim, tour museums, or just plain sightsee, your drive will take longer.

The drive begins in Lewisburg at the junction of US 219 and US 60, just off I–64 exit 169. It connects in Lewisburg with Drive 21, a 52-mile drive between Athens (near Princeton) and Lewisburg. The historic town of Lewisburg was established in 1782 and today features more than seventy eighteenth- and nineteenth-century historic building and sites.

Before leaving the area, consider a visit to Lost World Caverns, a commercial cave known for its huge rooms, totem pole-like stalagmites, and other large and gleaming calcite formations. To start on the drive immediately, skip the next three paragraphs and drive north on US 219. To reach the cave go north on Court Street from downtown, which becomes Fairview Drive, and follow the signs, which lead to the cave in about 1.5 miles.

EXPLORING LOST WORLD CAVERNS

When the cave was discovered in 1942, the only way in was a 120-foot rappel or rope ladder descent from the bottom of a grapevine-covered sinkhole. (And the way out entailed a 120-foot climb up to the sinkhole.) Known then as Grapevine Cave, for the next twenty-nine years it was visited only by the hardiest and most skilled cavers. To develop the cave for the public, a sloping access tunnel was drilled in 1971. Electric lighting and walkways were installed underground, with additional improvements on the surface, and the cave was renamed. Today the self-guiding tour, for which a fee is charged, leads over walkways and boardwalks through the largest rooms in the cave past the magnificent stalactites, stalagmites, flowstone, and other formations. Even with these improvements the trip entails almost constant climbing up and down numerous stairs and ramps and may be too strenuous for some.

The main room—the largest cave room open to the public east of Carlsbad Caverns—is more than 300 feet long and 50 feet wide, with a ceiling that arches more than 100 feet overhead. At one point you can look straight up twelve stories to a tiny pinpoint of light that marks the original natural entrance. The cave, a Registered National Landmark, is one of more than a thousand caves in the surrounding area.

If a tour on boardwalks is too tame for you, ask about guided tours to some of the primitive areas of the cave beyond the developed section, which have no walkways, no electric lights, and much mud and scrambling. Hardhats and headlamps are supplied. In one of these back passages bones of an extinct Pleistocene bear (*Arctotus pristinus*) were discovered.

When you're ready to begin the actual drive, go north on US 219 from Lewisburg, crossing under I-64. The Greenbrier Valley here is broad and open, dotted with farms, large herds of cattle, and verdant low hills.

Paralleling US 219 a mile or two to the east (right) are the Greenbrier River and the Greenbrier River Trail State Park. The Greenbrier River Trail follows the river and US 219 for 75 miles from Caldwell, east of Lewisburg, north to Cass. The packed dirt trail follows a former C&O railroad bed over thirty-five bridges and through two tunnels. The first trains, loaded with timber, puffed along the tracks here in 1900; there was a "First Train" celebration and fair in Marlinton. As the timber boom slowly ended, the branch line became a route for traffic between eastern and western cities. By the 1970s the branch was losing money, and the last trains rolled through in 1978.

The railroad donated the right-of-way to the state to be used as a trail, with the provision that it be maintained for future railroad use. Funding and development were slow at first, with flood damage creating additional problems. The trail was named the state's Millennium Legacy Trail in 2000, with a Hundred-Year Celebration in Marlinton.

Voted one of the ten best hiking trails in the country, its gentle grades—less than 1 percent—are favored by equestrians, novice bikers, and families with children. Fishing—the river is known for its trout—canoeing, and just floating on tubes down the clean Greenbrier River provide enjoyable respites from hiking and biking. Cross-country skiing is popular in winter.

The Greenbrier River Trail is accessible from several points along the drive; at side roads and intersections along US 219 look for signs directing you to the trail. For a taste of the trail, turn right on WV 11 in Renick, about 10 miles from Lewisburg. The parking area and trail access are just before the bridge about half a mile from US 219. If you visit in springtime, hike north along the trail for a mile or two to view trillium, redbud, and other wildflowers. Islands in the river form shallow feeding grounds for migratory fowl, including wood ducks and Canada geese, making this section a choice destination for bird watchers.

Most through hikers and bikers traverse the trail from north to south, following the slight downhill grade of the trail and the river. On foot the entire 80-mile trail can be covered in five or six days; astride a horse or a bike, it takes two or three days.

After visiting the trail return to US 219 and turn north (right). As you drive north the valley gradually narrows, and hardwood forests predominate over farmlands. A few minor hills, tame by West Virginia standards, add interest. About 21 miles from Lewisburg, just past the Pocahontas-Greenbrier County boundary, look for the sign on the right for Beartown State Park. (Use caution; this is an abrupt and acute right turn.) Follow the side road to the parking lot at Beartown State Park.

BEARTOWN'S NOOKS AND CRANNIES

At 110 acres, Beartown State Park is one of the smallest parks in the state. But this meandering labyrinth of house-sized boulders arouses awe and amazement in many. The rock, known as Droop or Pottsville sandstone, was originally deposited along the edge of ancient seas. For several thousand years the rock has been exposed along the ridge of Droop Mountain, and it has slowly eroded, weathered, and split along vertical joints or cracks in the sandstone. This has formed a multitude of fissures wide enough to walk through, many of them 30 to 50 feet deep, in the surrounding towers of boulders.

A half-mile-long boardwalk leads up, over, under, down, and around through this maze of rocks. A forest of hemlock, oak, and other hardwoods forms a thick canopy of leaves overhead, and ferns and mosses cover the forest floor and sprout from almost every tiny crack in the rock. Lichens grow where the ferns and mosses do not, to form gray blankets on the bare rock. Some elephant ear lichens are 5 feet across and more than a hundred years old. It's almost always damp and misty here, adding to the sense of timelessness and wonderment. Be forewarned: Many people visit here expecting to stay a half an hour but end up staying all day.

Bears are not especially common at Beartown. But early settlers *thought* that the huge boulders would be a good place for bears to live, and the name stuck. The gate to the parking area is locked from November through March, but you can hike in. Because this is an extremely fragile ecological area, you must stay on the boardwalk. There is no fee.

THE STATE'S LARGEST
CIVIL WAR CONFLICT

When you leave, turn around and return to US 219. Turn right (north). About 6 miles from Beartown on the left is Droop Mountain Battlefield State Park. The park is the site of West Virginia's largest Civil War conflict; 7,000 soldiers fought here on November 6, 1863. It was a decisive victory for the Union, causing the Confederate troops to retreat south into Virginia and ensuring that West Virginia would remain under federal control. The battle cost 600 men their lives; most of them were buried here. A museum contains artifacts and exhibits, including an account of the battle in the November 21, 1863, edition of the *New York Times*.

Whether you tour the battlefield or not, be sure to stop at the observation tower for views of the Greenbrier River Valley. Several short hiking trails lead to places of historic and scenic interest.

From Droop Mountain, continue north on US 219. After a few miles you reach the town of Hillsboro, where the general store stocks everything from old fashioned ice cream to horse plows to hiking supplies.

At Droop Mountain 7,000 soldiers fought near this observation tower.

The Sydenstricker House, Pearl Buck's birthplace, is now a museum.

Just past town on the left is the restored Pearl S. Buck Museum and birthplace of the famed author. The large house was built by her maternal grandparents, the Stultings, in the 1870s as a replica of their former home in Holland; many of the furnishings reflect the styles of that period.

Buck was the daughter of Presbyterian missionaries stationed in China. Her parents had lost three of their four children before Pearl was born; they returned to her maternal grandparents' home for her birth. She was born in 1892 as Pearl Comfort Sydenstricker. A few months after her birth she returned with her parents to China. Except for four years at Randolph-Macon Women's College in Virginia and a postgraduate year at Cornell University in New York, she spent the first forty years of her life in China.

A prolific writer, Buck wrote some eighty-five books, including novels, numerous short stories, children's books, translations from the Chinese, poetry, and essays. The years she lived in China are reflected in many of her works. She received the Pulitzer Prize for her second and best-known novel, *The Good Earth*, the first of a trilogy about a Chinese family. The book sold more than 1.8 million copies in 1931, the year it was published, and was translated into thirty languages. In 1938 she was awarded the Nobel Prize in Literature, the only woman to win both prizes.

Buck returned to the United Sates in 1934, where she settled in Pennsylvania and married her publisher and second husband, Richard Welsh. Until her death in 1973 she continued to write and publish and was active in civil rights and women's rights groups. She established and endowed an agency for the adoption of Asian-American children. She was acutely aware of the ambiguities of her childhood and life and her attempts to reconcile her two worlds. Her several biographical books about her parents showed Buck's strong affection and emotional ties to the hills of West Virginia.

Costumed guides provide tours of the Stulting House. In addition to her grandparents' furnishings, the building is a partial repository for her manuscripts, papers, and books; the rest are stored at Randolph-Macon Women's College. The smaller building to the left of the manor house is a reconstruction of her father's home in Greenbrier County. Known as the Sydenstricker House, it functions as a gift shop and bookstore. Many first editions and signed copies of her works are available. The facility is open from May to October. An admission fee is charged.

WATOGA, RIVER OF THE ISLANDS

A few miles north of the Buck museum on US 219 a sign directs you to wooded and hilly Watoga State Park, about 2 miles south (right) on WV 27 and just across the Greenbrier River and Greenbrier Trail. At 10,100 acres Watoga is the largest state park in West Virginia and is one of the most popular, with hiking, boating, fishing, and camping among the main activities. In the Cherokee language, the park's name means "river of the islands," which aptly describes the numerous shallows, low islands, and sandbars along this stretch of the Greenbrier.

Fishing, boating, and swimming are prime activities, both in the river and in an eleven-acre lake. Two campgrounds provide more than ninety campsites, and there are several rental cabins. Numerous trails lead through the woods and arboretum. For day users several picnic areas provide attractive places to sup, particularly the T. M. Cheek site atop one of the highest ridges in the park. If you want more pampered dining, try the park's restaurant. During the summer months rangers schedule a variety of nature walks, hikes, and other activities. Ask the rangers how to see the old bank safe still in place in the former town of Watoga along the Greenbrier River Trail.

Most of the park's facilities lie in the northern half of the park; the southern section, popular with wilderness hikers, borders undeveloped Calvin Price State Forest and the Monongahela National Forest. The park is open from April through December, with limited facilities accessible in winter.

From Watoga, it is about 14 miles north on US 219 to Marlinton. At the restored 1904 building that houses the Pocahontas County Historical Museum in Marlinton are many exhibits and photographs of Marlinton's rich history, including Indian artifacts, Civil War memorabilia, and railroad and timber industry displays, plus early farm equipment, washing machines, and other household appliances. Of course there are several books by Pearl S. Buck, many signed by the author. On the museum grounds is an 1840 log cabin. Nearby is the handsome Marlinton Railroad Depot, restored for the Hundred Year Millennium in 2000.

Marlinton is the end of this drive. The Greenbrier River Trail continues north about 25 miles to terminate in Cass (via US 219 and WV 1 by vehicle). Cass is near the starting point for Drive 16, Railroad Loop and the NRAO. About 7 miles north of Marlinton on US 219 is one end of the Drive 15, Highland Scenic Byway.

19

Thurmond Depot

AT THE BOTTOM OF THE NEW RIVER GORGE

GENERAL DESCRIPTION: The drive descends into the New River Gorge to the historic railroad town of Thurmond for views of the old town and the New River, then returns via the same route for a 20-mile trip. An optional drive for four-wheel-drive vehicles on dirt roads continues along the New River for another 13 miles for a 23-mile trip.

LOCATION: South-central West Virginia.

SPECIAL ATTRACTIONS: The historic railroad depot and town of Thurmond, in the New River Gorge National River, the New River itself, and the New River Gorge.

DRIVING ROUTE NUMBERS AND NAME: WV 25, also known as the McKendree Road.

TRAVEL SEASON: Late spring through November. Visitation is heaviest in late October when the fall colors are at their best and on weekends in the spring and fall.

CAMPING: Some primitive camping is allowed on National Park Service property; check with the Park Service for restrictions. Plum Orchard Lake Wildlife Management Area west of Glen Jean has forty rustic campsites. Babcock State Park east of the drive has more than 50 standard campsites. South of Fayetteville are more than half a dozen private campgrounds.

SERVICES: No automotive services are available along the drive. A snack and souvenir store is usually open at Thurmond during the warmer months.

NEARBY ATTRACTIONS: Grandview State Park, Babcock State Park, Canyon Rim Visitor Center (see Drive 17), and Tamarack.

THE DRIVE

Thurmond Depot, a part of the New River Gorge National River, is a restored coal-shipping railroad town at the bottom of the New River Gorge. This drive, along WV 25, follows along a narrow and winding two-lane paved road from Glen Jean 10 miles into the gorge to Thurmond. There you

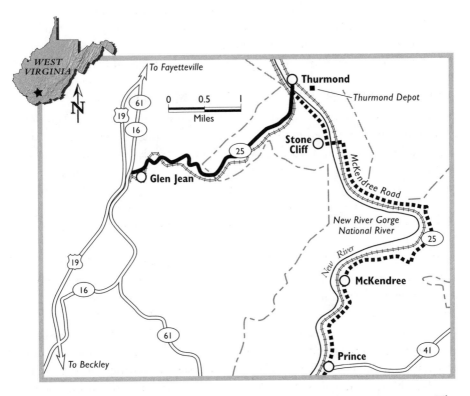

can tour the old town by yourself or with National Park Service rangers. The drive is steep and not recommended for trailers.

From Thurmond an unimproved dirt road leads along the New River another 13 miles past numerous former mining camps to emerge on WV 41 near Grandview State Park; this makes a total trip of about 23 miles. This optional portion of the drive is recommended only for four-wheel-drive vehicles and others equipped for backcountry travel. If, like most visitors, you decide not to take this portion of the drive, you will have to retrace the drive back to Glen Jean. For that trip, the total mileage is about 20 miles.

Steam-driven railroads powered by coal made Thurmond a boomtown in the 1880s, and diesel-driven trains turned it into a near-ghost town fifty years later. In the early 1870s, Thurmond was a sleepy settlement on a bend at the bottom of the New River Gorge. A few small coal mines enabled the residents to eke out a marginal existence.

Elsewhere the Industrial Revolution was bringing sweeping economic and social changes. The booming railroad industry, powered by coal-using steam engines, was bringing swift and economical transportation to many areas of the country. In 1873 the Chesapeake & Ohio Railroad main line was completed through the New River Gorge. Steam-driven trains began to rumble through Thurmond, carrying coal to blast furnaces in eastern cities that produced iron around the clock to satisfy the demands of the growing nation.

BOOM AND BUST IN THURMOND

At first Thurmond was little more than a watering stop for the trains. As more coal mines were developed in the area, the town became a shipping and loading area for the trains headed east. Water tanks and coal loading towers were built, along with a passenger depot and engine house. Soon houses dotted the steep slopes of the gorge, and to service them the town sported hotels, banks, stores and restaurants—even a meat packing plant. So narrow was the gorge that the town had no streets, just the railroad tracks running past the main business block.

By the early 1900s the railroads directly employed more than 100 people, with 300 more working for other businesses. Fourteen passenger and countless coal trains stopped in town daily. With coal as its mainstay, the town generated some 20 percent of all C&O revenue.

The boom years ended in a whimper. In the 1930s the Depression enveloped the country and all business slowed down. Trains still came through town, but not quite as often. Traffic increased slightly during World War II. The final blow came when the C&O replaced its coal-fired locomotives with diesels. Thurmond was no longer needed, and the town virtually disappeared.

Or did it? For many years Thurmond was a near-ghost town. After World War II, as the interstate highway system was developed, visitors began to rediscover West Virginia's previously hidden charms and rugged beauty. Hikers, bikers, cavers, skiers, anglers, hunters, and just plain sightseers came to visit. The Gauley, New, and Cheat Rivers were fearlessly traversed by white-water enthusiasts who recognized them as world-class rapids. In 1977 the New River Bridge (see Drive 17) was opened, cutting travel time by an hour or more to many areas.

NEW RIVER JOINS THE NATIONAL PARK SYSTEM

And in 1978 Congress added the New River Gorge National River to the National Park System, preserving Thurmond and fifty miles of the New

Thurmond Depot restored to its former glory.

River for all time. Renovations and improvements followed national park status, including restoration of the Thurmond Depot and much of the town to look as it did in the 1930s. Thousands of visitors now flock to the town—not to work, but to view the restored depot and town, raft down the New River, or hike the trails.

To begin the drive take the Glen Jean exit from US 19 at the intersection of WV 16/61 and WV 25. Signs point the way east on WV 25 to Thurmond and the New River Gorge.

Town is soon left behind. The road parallels a creek and railroad track as it curves its way down to the gorge, past woods, small groups of houses, and several one-lane bridges. The tracks and railroad siding are still in use to haul coal from a small mine. After a few miles you pass the boundary into the New River Gorge National River. Just beyond is the trailhead for the Thurmond-Minden Trail, an easy hiking and biking trail 3.4 miles one way that leads along an old railroad bed to the town of Minden, north of Glen Jean. A small waterfall is one of the highlights of the hike, plus views of both Thurmond and Minden.

As you reach the bottom of the gorge, signs will direct you to parking. The small amount of level ground, plus heavy summer weekend visitation, has

Freight and passenger trains still rumble through Thurmond on the main line of the CSX.

forced the Park Service to create satellite parking areas. If travel is light, you may be able to drive across the combined railroad bridge and one-lane auto bridge across the New River to Thurmond; otherwise you can walk or take a shuttle bus to the depot.

Either way there are good views of the river, which can be a placid stream or a roaring torrent. If the latter, look for white-water rafters as they float under the bridge.

At Thurmond your first stop should be the railroad depot just before town, where during the warmer months rangers lead tours of the Thurmond historical district. They can also help you plan a walk or hike along several trails in the vicinity.

Trains still run here, and the tracks, which are private property, are still the main line of the CSX, successor to the C&O Railroad. Coal and freight trains still rumble through the gorge, now pulled by powerful modern diesel engines. Amtrak's crack passenger train, the Cardinal, passes through several times a week on its run between Washington, D. C., and Chicago. Rail enthusiasts plan for months to be aboard the special excursion trains that run when the fall color is at its best. Check with Amtrak (see the Appendix) for more information.

For most vehicles Thurmond is as far as you can go, and you will have to turn around and retrace the drive back to Glen Jean. You may be able to drive another 3 miles south along the New River to Stone Cliff, which, when the road is open, is a popular picnic, fishing, hiking, and swimming area. You'll also see the cliffs that give this spot its name.

But Thurmond or Stone Cliff is the end for most vehicles. If you have a four-wheel-drive or high-centered vehicle, ask the rangers if the McKendree Road is passable. This road, a continuation of WV 25, is reached by crossing the New River via the low bridge at Stone Cliff and following the dirt road on the other side. The road passes by several old mining camps, including McKendree, but little remains except a few houses.

This section of the drive ends at Prince at the intersection with WV 41. To return to Glen Jean, turn west (right) on WV 41, and then north (right again) at WV 61 back to Glen Jean.

Hatfield~McCoy country

MOUNTAIN FEUDS AND COALFIELDS

GENERAL DESCRIPTION: A 55-mile drive along the scenic Tug Fork River to Matewan, scene of the Hatfield-McCoy feuds, and then past hilly and curvy coal country to Logan.

SPECIAL ATTRACTIONS: Coal House, Tug Fork River, Matewan and the Hatfield-McCoy story, and coal mines.

LOCATION: Southwest West Virginia on the Kentucky border.

DRIVING ROUTE NUMBERS AND NAME: US 52, 119, WV 44, CR 49, 52.

TRAVEL SEASON: All year.

CAMPING: Laurel Creek Wildlife Management Area, north of Williamson, has twenty-five tent sites; Chief Logan State Park has twenty-five sites with hookups.

SERVICES: All at Williamson and Logan; limited at Matewan.

NEARBY ATTRACTIONS: Chief Logan State Park and Laurel Creek Wildlife Management Area.

THE DRIVE

It's rough country in the southwestern corner of the state. The land is all up and down. Roads, except for a few major highways, go up and down, too. Roads also go left, right, and around, with more curves than straightaways.

In 1890 Williamson was farmland, one of the few flat areas among the hills. As railroads were built to haul coal from the numerous productive mines, the city grew and flourished as a rail and commercial center. Today coal is not quite the king it was a hundred years ago, but the city still maintains its economic importance.

Decades of coal mining have left their mark on the land, but in recent years recreation and tourism have been recognized as being perhaps as important as mining. As tourism has grown, interest has been regenerated in the most infamous feud in the country, between the Hatfields and McCoys, which took place in Matewan.

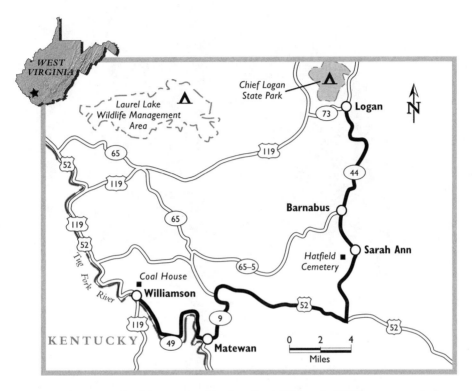

On this 55-mile drive, you visit the Coal House in Williamson and then follow the meandering Tug Fork of the Big Sandy River to Matewan, scene of the infamous Hatfield-McCoy feud. From there, the drive goes past coal mines and coal towns to end at Logan near Chief Logan State Park.

The drive begins by the courthouse square in Williamson, at perhaps the most beautiful building in Mingo County: the licorice-black Coal House. Built entirely of coal, the building is a testimony to coal's importance to the region's economy, history, and social structure.

THE COAL HOUSE

The shiny black rectangular building with its graceful entrance and window arches was built in 1933 at the height of the Depression entirely from donations. Local coal, sixty-five tons of it, was carefully cut into blocks and shaped with hand tools. To maintain a uniform black appearance, the mortar was mixed with lampblack. The seventy-year-old building is protected from the weather and kept in top condition by a coat of shellac every two years.

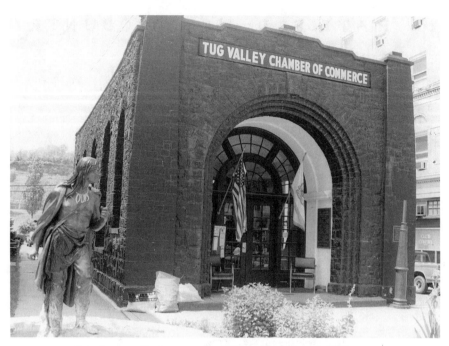

Sixty-five tons of coal were used to build the Coal House in Williamson,
now home to the Tug Valley Chamber of Commerce.

The structure is the home of the Tug Valley Chamber of Commerce, which can give you information on other points of interest in the area. Don't be afraid to go inside; the coal won't ignite (but no smoking, please).

From Williamson go east on US 52 past the huge railyard. You may see a train or two of coal cars today, but years ago this yard would have been filled to capacity with long trains laden down with coal. About 1 mile from town, turn right on WV 49. The road and adjacent railroad follow the many twists and turns of the West Virginia side of the Tug Fork of the Big Sandy River, with views of the steep Kentucky banks across the water. Active coal mines are just off this road, so be alert for coal trucks.

After 15 miles of bends, you reach Matewan (pronounced MATE wan), which has a history larger than the town. The town became notorious in 1882 when three sons of Randolph McCoy stabbed and shot Ellison Hatfield, brother of Devil Anse Hatfield, in Pike County, Kentucky. Ellison was carried across the Tug Fork to Matewan, where he died. Devil Anse, patriarch of the Hatfield family, immediately retaliated by executing the three McCoys in Kentucky just across the river from Matewan.

Coal is brought from the mine via the conveyer transporter on the hillside to this station to be loaded into trucks or railroad cars.

MATEWAN'S BLOODY HISTORY

West Virginia bounty hunters rode into Kentucky to capture the Hatfields. The feud continued on both sides of the river for another ten years, with retaliatory murders in both families. Why the three McCoy brothers killed Ellison is not known. But the story was sensationalized in national news for years, helping to spawn the image of a violent and backward Appalachia that still lingers today.

Forty years later in 1920, Matewan was again the site of violence, this time between townspeople, miners, and mine company detectives. At that time the United Mine Workers were attempting to unionize the local coal miners. However, those who joined were summarily fired and evicted from their company-owned homes. In a dramatic showdown Chief of Police Sid Hatfield and Mayor Cable Testermen confronted company-hired detectives who were evicting miners. An argument and shots ensued, leaving the mayor, seven detectives, and three miners dead in the massacre.

Hatfield became a hero to the miners and was acquitted of murder charges. But a year later he and a union activist were murdered by revenge-bent detectives on the steps of the courthouse in Welch. (Drive 23, Coal Heritage Trail, visits Welch.)

Matewan was founded in 1897 when the Norfolk and Western Railway opened a main line to serve the Williamson Coalfield. The town serviced the surrounding mining communities; its saloons were gathering places for miners and railroad workers to gamble and carouse.

The town today, one block long, is peaceful enough, and, in 1997, was the first area in the coalfields to be designated a National Historic Landmark. Stop at the Matewan Development Center in the Hatfield Building (next to the McCoy Building) for a map and guide. Don't miss the Old Matewan National Bank Building, with bullet holes still visible from the 1920 massacre. A recording by the bank describes the event, including recollections of elderly residents who experienced the shootings and trials first-hand. The town is also a stop along the Hatfield-McCoy Bike Trail.

The feud still goes on but is somewhat friendlier, with a Hatfield-McCoy festival each spring. A highlight is a tug of war over the Tug Fork, with the Hatfields in Kentucky and the McCoys in West Virginia. The losing team gets dragged into the next state (if the river is low enough).

When you leave town, go left on WV 65 (shown as WV 9 on some maps). The road climbs out of the river valley and ends at US 52. Turn right (south). It's slow going on this curvy road, even though it is a major route.

Devil Anse stands tall over the Hatfield family grave at Sara Ann.
Photo: Courtesy West Virginia State Archives.

DEVIL ANSE'S FINAL RESTING SPOT

Turn left (north) on WV 44. In Sarah Ann you pass the Hatfield Family Cemetery, also on the National Register of Historic Places, which has a life-sized Italian marble statue of patriarch Devil Anse Hatfield. A survivor of the feuds, Devil Anse died of old age.

Coal continues to be a major economic force in southern West Virginia, and the drive passes through several small mining communities and mines. Look for reconditioned land on former hilltops where the coal has been removed and the land reclaimed. This controversial mining method still continues because surface mines are more economical than underground mining.

The drive ends at Logan. Nearby is Chief Logan State Park, close enough to town so that residents can come here evenings for a walk along the Guyandotte Beauty Trail or a game of miniature golf. In summer productions of the Aracoma Story are staged. This play tells the story of Aracoma, daughter of a Shawnee Indian chief who married a captured British soldier; the soldier later became a chief himself. A twenty-five-site campground is open all year.

From Logan it is a few miles to US 119, a four-lane modern highway that will zip you south back to Williamson or north to Charleston.

Athens to Lewisburg

BLUESTONE GORGE AND LAKE AND PENCE SPRINGS

GENERAL DESCRIPTION: A 52-mile drive past a 900-foot-deep gorge and then along the meandering Greenbrier River. The drive passes steep gorges, scenic lakes, extensive caves, and historic buildings and towns.

SPECIAL ATTRACTIONS: Pipestem State Park, Bluestone National Scenic River, Bluestone State Park, Bluestone Lake and Dam, historic Hinton, John Henry monument, Pence Springs, Organ Cave, and Lewisburg.

LOCATION: Southern West Virginia.

DRIVING ROUTE NUMBERS AND NAME: US 219; WV 3, 20, 63.

TRAVEL SEASON: All year.

CAMPING: Camping is available all year at Bluestone and Pipestem State Parks, with more than a hundred sites with hookups and all conveniences. Private campgrounds near Pipestem, Hinton, Alderson, and True are open during the warmer months.

SERVICES: All services are available in most towns along the drive.

NEARBY ATTRACTIONS: Sandstone Falls, New River Gorge National River, and Organ Cave.

THE DRIVE

From the rolling plateau country near Princeton in southern West Virginia, this 52-mile drive takes you to Pipestem State Park for views of the 900-foot-deep gorge of the Bluestone National Scenic River and the many recreational facilities along Bluestone Lake. From there the drive passes historic Hinton, gateway to the New River Gorge National River. It then follows the winding Greenbrier River past the monument to John Henry of folklore fame to the inn and springs at Pence Springs.

The drive continues along the Greenbrier River, passing near Organ Cave, the largest in West Virginia, to end at Lewisburg, another historic town. The drive is over paved highways and can be made at any time.

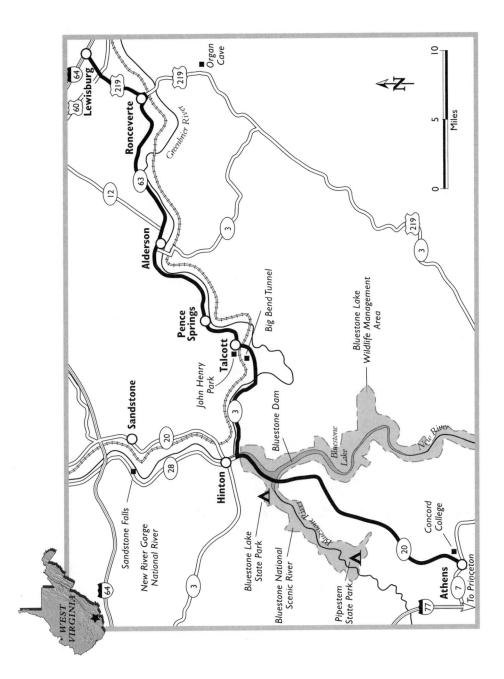

Begin at Athens, just north of Princeton via WV 20. Or, from I–77 north of Princeton, take exit 14-WV 7, to WV 20. Athens is home of Concord College, one of West Virginia's many fine small private colleges. If your timing is right, you will hear the bells of its world-class carillon ring out over the campus. These melodious sounds result from a gift by former Concord president Joseph Marsh. As a Dartmouth College alumnus, Dr. Marsh fondly recalled the sonorous Baker Library bells of his alma mater. When he retired, his generous gift provided funding for the Concord carillon.

From Athens drive north on WV 20 through mixed woods and farmland. Note the drive-in theater, one of the few operating ones left in the state. About 13 miles from Athens is the entrance to Pipestem State Park, perched on the rim of the 1,000-foot gorge of the Bluestone River. You can see much of the gorge from several scenic overlooks and an observation tower, but if you have the time, ride the aerial tramway to the bottom of the gorge for an unforgettable skyway experience.

If superb scenery and a tramway aren't enough, this park offers recreational activities for just about everybody: fishing, swimming, hiking trails, outdoor concerts, horseback riding, tennis, nature walks and, in winter, cross-country skiing. Two lodges—one on the rim, another at the bottom—a campground, cottages, and several restaurants cater to all tastes.

The 4,000-acre park lies almost entirely within the boundaries of the Bluestone National Scenic River. Almost unspoiled, the bottom of the Bluestone River gorge has no roads and no trains, just hiking and horse trails that lead from the lodge. The river gets its name from the blue or gray shale exposed in the gorge. And the pipestem bush, which gives the park its name, is a hollow woody shrub used by American Indians to make pipes.

When you leave Pipestem, turn left and continue north on WV 20. The road, which has been more or less level, begins a long, gradual descent almost to river level. It crosses the Bluestone River on a high bridge at its confluence with the New River.

BLUESTONE'S LAKE AND PARKS

Past the bridge is the entrance to Bluestone Lake State Park, which has a boat launch area, a campground, and some rental cabins. Both rivers combine here to form Bluestone Lake, impounded by Bluestone Dam, which you will pass in a few minutes. The 2,000-acre elongated lake is part of yet another "Bluestone," Bluestone Lake Wildlife Management Area.

As you might guess, water activities are popular, with excellent fishing for largemouth and smallmouth bass, crappie, and catfish. On warm weekends you'll

*Bluestone Dam in Hinton rises 165 feet to form Bluestone Lake,
which is popular for boating and fishing.*

see sailboats, powerboats, canoes, fishermen, and water skiers, with more anglers along the shore. The road, about 75 feet above the lake, is a good vantage point for these activities.

Ahead is the massive Bluestone Dam. This concrete structure rises 165 feet above the riverbed and spans 2,048 feet across the river. Built by the U.S. Army Corps of Engineers, construction began in 1942, but with the intervention of World War II, it was not finished until 1952.

The dam's original purpose was for flood control, but the lake soon developed into a major recreational resource. Its national significance was recognized in 1978 when the New River Gorge National River, stretching north of Hinton for 53 miles, was added to the National Park system. Drives 17 and 19 descend into the New River Gorge to explore this parkland. In 1988 the Bluestone National Scenic River was created, followed by the plethora of other "Bluestone" facilities.

Wheelchair-accessible tours of the dam start at the visitor center on top of the structure several days a week from Memorial Day through Labor Day. About half a mile past the dam, turn east (right) on WV 3, crossing the New River on the Bellepoint Bridge where the Greenbrier River flows into the New.

The town of Hinton, gateway to both the Bluestone National Scenic River and the New River Gorge National River, lies to the left after you cross the bridge. Hinton's historic district, with churches, homes, and businesses dating from the railroad and coal mining boom years of the late 1800s, includes several varieties of eclectic Victorian architecture. Also in town is a National Park Visitor Center. Ask the rangers about a side trip to Sandstone Falls north of town on WV 26. Railroad buffs may enjoy a stop at the Hinton Railroad Museum.

From Hinton, WV 3 follows the valley of the winding Greenbrier River, occasionally taking a shortcut over low hills while the river flows serenely below in wide bends and curves. As you come down the hill before Talcott, look for a sign and small park on the right. At the park overlooking the town is a larger-than-life statue of a bare-chested black man with a hammer in his arms. This is that steel drivin' man, John Henry, who looks ready to pound more steel. Down below, railroad tracks disappear beneath you into the 6,500-foot Big Bend Tunnel.

Folk songs and folklore aside, historians report that a 200-pound black man and freed slave named John Henry did indeed help dig the tunnel for the Chesapeake and Ohio Railroad in the 1870s. But did John Henry die trying to outwork a steam drill? Probably not; more likely he was one of many killed by numerous rockfalls in the soft shale during the building of the tunnel.

John Henry, hammer in hand, looks ready to drive more steel.

From the bottom of the hill, look back to see the portal for the original tunnel and the modern replacement with tracks. Talcott is proud of its John Henry heritage and celebrates his memory with a festival each spring.

PENCE SPRINGS HOTEL AND SPA

A few bends beyond Talcott is the small town of Pence Springs. In 1872 Andrew Pence built a hotel by the spring site and began selling the sulphur-rich mineral water. Business was slow for many years until 1904, when the Pence Springs bottled water won a silver medal at the St. Louis World's Fair. Soon Andrew Pence was shipping several railcars a week of his water. The original hotel burned down a few years later, but Pence rebuilt in style, including such modern conveniences as telephones and showers in each room, a central vacuum system, and special accommodations for chauffeurs and maids.

Known as the Grand Hotel, it became the most expensive and most popular hotel in West Virginia, as well-heeled travelers from around the world came for relaxation, entertainment, and to imbibe the strong-tasting water. When Prohibition came along, a hidden cellar kept liquor flowing along with the spring water, attracting gamblers from an adjacent casino who came to celebrate or mourn their luck.

But as the Depression deepened, even bootleg liquor was not enough to keep the hotel going, and it closed in the early 1930s. The building reopened later as a school for girls, and when that enterprise was not successful, it became a dude ranch. In 1944 the state bought the property and after renovations used it for the next forty years as the maximum-security state prison for women. How the prisoners felt about being locked up in a formerly posh resort hotel is not known.

In the early 1980s the property and springs was bought by Ashby Berkley, who, as son of a prison worker, grew up on the premises. After meticulous renovations, Berkley reopened it in 1986 as the present Pence Springs Hotel. Today's inn, run by John and Wendy Lincoln, has simple rooms. It is a place to relax, play horseshoes or croquet, go hiking on the 400-acre grounds, or go fishing or canoeing in the adjacent Greenbrier River. The inn and spring house are now on the National Register of Historic Places.

A few remnants of prison life remain: peepholes in the doors, but with the covers now on the inside; and, if you ask, the staff will show you the solitary confinement cells, still encaged in heavy steel bars and doors. And the spring continues to bubble forth its tasteful liquid, with plans to resume bottling the once-famous water.

*The Pence Springs Hotel—from hotel to prison to school and back to hotel—
has been meticulously restored.*

From Pence Springs WV 12 continues to follow the tranquil and meandering Greenbrier River. At Alderson, a pleasant residential town lying partly in three different counties, the river is spanned by the stone arch of Memorial Bridge, built in 1914 and now open only to pedestrian traffic.

Bear right on WV 63 as you leave Alderson. At the intersection with US 219 in Ronceverte (French for "Greenbrier") go north (left) on US 219. For a side trip to Organ Cave, the state's largest and one of its most historic caves, follow US 219 about 4 miles to the cave.

ORGAN CAVE'S UNDERGROUND WONDERS

A National Natural Landmark, the cave is probably best known for its use during the War of 1812 and the Civil War as a source of saltpeter, from which gunpowder was made. Numerous vats used for leaching the dirt, and other equipment used to mine saltpeter, are in an excellent state of preservation and can be seen along the tour.

The cave has been known to European settlers since 1704. Explorations keep extending its more than 40 miles of passages. When Thomas Jefferson visited the cave in the late 1700s, he discovered several fossils. Since then the cave has proven to be a rich trove of Pleistocene and Pliocene mammal fossils, including such extinct species as the saber-toothed cat, caribou, and American mastodon.

Guided tours today take you past many of the historical areas, through large rooms, and past colorful and impressive formations such as the namesake Organ. All-day tours can be arranged into some of the undeveloped portions of the cave.

From Ronceverte, take US 219 north past the State Fair of West Virginia; this annual event each August attracts more than 250,000 visitors. The fairgrounds are on the outskirts of Lewisburg, which was settled around 1750 and is one of the oldest towns in the state. It has many buildings preserved in the historic district from the 1700s and 1800s. A walking tour will take you past the Old Stone Church, constructed in 1796 and the oldest church west of the Alleghenies in continuous use, and Carnegie Hall, built in 1902 with a gift from Andrew Carnegie.

This 52-mile drive ends in Lewisburg, off exit 169 of I–64. Drive 18 continues north along the Greenbrier River.

22

Farm Heritage Road Scenic Byway

FARMS AND THE SPAS OF YESTERDAY

GENERAL DESCRIPTION: A 60-mile drive, part of the National Scenic Byway System, that has changed little in the last hundred years. The drive goes past farms, nineteenth-century springs and resorts, historic towns and buildings, and mountain scenery.

SPECIAL ATTRACTIONS: Several former major spas and resorts, Indian Creek Covered Bridge, restored and historical Union, Rehoboth Church, Sweetsprings Valley, and Peters Mountain.

LOCATION: Southern West Virginia, southwest of White Sulphur Springs and I-64.

DRIVING ROUTE NUMBERS AND NAME: US 219; WV 3, 12, 122.

TRAVEL SEASON: All year. In spring redbuds jump into bloom as the trees slowly become clothed in green. In fall the same leaves bathe the mountainsides in shades

of yellow, red, and orange. Occasional winter snowstorms coat the hills and woods in white.

CAMPING: Moncove Lake State Park just off the drive near Gap Mills has about fifty campsites, half with complete facilities. Bluestone State Park and Bluestone Lake Wildlife Management Area west of the drive together have more than 400 campsites; about 100 have complete facilities. Wilderness camping is permitted in the Jefferson National Forest east of Gap Mills.

SERVICES: Gasoline and food are available in towns along the drive.

NEARBY ATTRACTIONS: Moncove State Park, Bluestone State Park, Bluestone Lake Wildlife Management Area, Organ Cave, Hanging Rock Observatory (hawk migrations), and Jefferson National Forest.

THE DRIVE

Follow the trail of the stage coaches a hundred years ago as they carried their passengers from resort to resort and spa to spa. Step back in time to when most people lived on farms or in small towns. The springs and spas of Monroe County once attracted thousands of visitors each year; the ailing who came seeking relief in the soothing mineral waters, and the rich who

Farm Heritage Road Scenic Byway

22 FARM HERITAGE ROAD SCENIC BYWAY

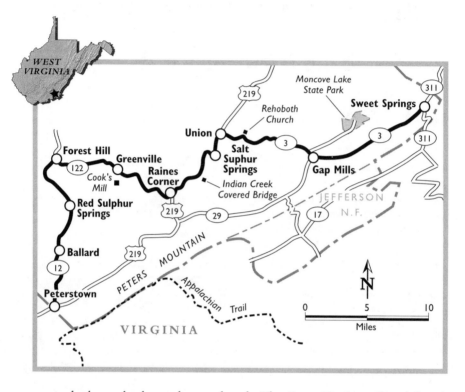

came to bathe and relax at luxury hotels. The Farm Heritage Road Scenic Byway in Monroe County visits several of these former resorts, as well as historic towns, a covered bridge, and the oldest church east of the Alleghenies. The drive combines both history and scenery in a rural America that is fast disappearing.

Begin in Peterstown on the Virginia border, at the junction of US 219 and WV 12. Peterstown, the largest town of any size along the drive, is sometimes known as West Virginia's diamond center. In fact the only and largest diamond ever found in the state was discovered here in 1928 by the Jones family while pitching horseshoes. At a hefty thirty-four carats the Jones diamond was large enough to get prospectors out scrambling for more. Geologists speculate that the diamond is an alluvial diamond, carried to its discovery point by streams, and that the source was to the south in Virginia. But the source—and another diamond—has never been found.

From Peterstown, go north on WV 12. The drive climbs gradually past gently rolling farmland. Look behind you to see the gap where the New River flows between Peters Mountain on the left and East River Mountain.

RED SULPHUR SPRINGS

At Red Sulphur Springs you come to the first of several former resorts and spas built at springs. The Red Sulphur Springs Hotel, built in 1832, was one of the most popular, with facilities for 550 visitors plus their horses and servants. Annual visits were touted as a means of maintaining good health. For those who were ailing, spring water was often seen as the remedy for all manner of afflictions. Publications in both medical and lay journals touted the benefits of taking the waters. Writing in the *Southern Literary Magazine* in 1835, T. W. White recommended Red Sulphur Springs water for pulmonary disease, hemorrhages, chills and fevers, asthma, consumption, night sweats, and a rapid pulse. It was not enough, he said, to bathe in it; readers were admonished to drink four quarts of spring water every twenty-four hours. Here is a brief quote to give you the flavor of his article:

> *In diseases of the liver, this water is highly efficacious. In dropsy, rheumatism, gravel, gout, dyspepsia, tic doloreux, and epilepsy, it has been used with advantage. In cutaneous diseases, it seldom fails to effect a cure.*

The hotel served as a military hospital during the Civil War. Like many of the springs, Red Sulphur never regained its former popularity after that. In part this was due to the hard times that followed the war. Springs also lost much of their medical appeal as people began to understand the contagious nature of many diseases and how close proximity to the ill may help to spread them. The hotel eventually closed, and nothing remains of its former glory today except the spring. Looking over the small community, you would not realize that it was once a major resort.

Turn right on WV 12 at the intersection with WV 122 in Forest Hill. Just before Greenville is the site of Cook's Fort, which covered more than an acre and reputedly protected more than 300 settlers from an Indian attack in 1778. Like the Red Sulphur Springs hotel, there are no remnants of the fort today. Still standing and restored to working order is Cook's Mill. The original mill operated in the early 1700s. The present building and water wheel were built in 1867, and renovations are still taking place. On summer weekends craftsmen and artisans demonstrate their skills.

Where there are springs and limestone, you usually find caves, and Monroe County has several hundred of these underground wonders. Some were mined for saltpeter in the early 1800s and during the Civil War. Chemically,

Cook's Mill, near Greenville and restored to working order, has craft demonstrations on weekends in the summer.

saltpeter is potassium nitrate, often found in cave dirt, and vital in frontier days for the manufacture of gunpowder. The "peter dirt" was stored in wooden hoppers and loaded onto mule-powered carts for removal. The wooden hoppers and cart tracks in the cave floor can still be seen in some caves.

WV 122 ends at the intersection with US 219. Turn north (left). If you've taken many other scenic drives in West Virginia, you may already have traveled on other parts of US 219. This U.S. highway runs northeast-southwest for some 150 miles past much of the state's prettiest mountain scenery along the Allegheny Front, from Peterstown, West Virginia, to Maryland. It follows the Seneca Trail or Warrior's Trail, an ancient American Indian pathway, through much of the southeast to New York.

INDIAN CREEK COVERED BRIDGE

A few miles along US 219 is the Indian Creek Covered Bridge at the side of the road near a sign and small parking area. The bridge should be memorialized as a monument to youthful labor and ingenuity. It was constructed around 1900 by the two Weikle brothers when they were still teenagers. In fair repair today, the 50-foot bridge is no longer used by highway traffic but is open for pedestrians.

Perhaps the Weikles built the bridge to ease the way for stagecoaches to reach Salt Sulphur Springs, just past the bridge. With many of the original buildings still standing, the Salt, as it was called, is one of the best preserved along the drive. When it opened in 1821 visitors had their choice of three types of springs: sulphur, sweet, and iodine. The main building, the Salt Sulphur Springs Hotel, was constructed in 1836 and is easily recognized by its Jeffersonian stately columns. Other structures still standing include a store, church, spring house, and bathhouse. Built from local limestone, this is the largest pre–Civil War stone complex in the state. It is privately owned, so tours are not available.

A few miles past the Salt is the town of Union, which also looks much as it did in the 1830s. Settled in 1774, it became the Monroe County seat in 1799. Some forty-six antebellum buildings are preserved in its historical district,

Built in 1786, Rehoboth Church near Union is the oldest church building west of the Allegheny Mountains, with gravestones dating to the early 1700s. What looks like the roof is a modern external structure to protect the church's original roof.

including an 1810 log house and one of the first black Methodist churches. Stop at the Monroe County Historical Society Museum for its historical displays and a self-guiding walking tour. The tour includes the Green Hill Cemetery, where soldiers from both the Revolutionary and Civil Wars are interred. Almost the entire town is on the National Register of Historic Places.

You may notice a monument with a statue of a soldier in a field outside the village. This is the 20-foot-high Monroe County Confederate Monument. More than 10,000 people attended the monument's dedication in 1901; it is topped by a statue of a Confederate soldier. The town fathers located it here, expecting that the town would soon grow around it, but it didn't, and the monument is still surrounded by cows and a cornfield.

REHOBOTH CHURCH, OLDEST WEST OF THE ALLEGHENIES

When you leave Union, turn east (right) on WV 3, leaving US 219. At 3 miles on the left is the Rehoboth Church. Finished in 1786, this small log building is the oldest church building west of the Alleghenies and one of ten dedicated Methodist shrines in the United States. What appears to be the roof is a modern external metal structure that protects the original wooden roof below. The adjacent cemetery dates from the 1700s. A small museum is open during the warmer months.

The rolling, hilly farmland between Union and Gap Mills has few surface streams; most of the drainage is underground. Rain water percolates into the limestone rock, picking up various minerals and impurities. The water later emerges at lower elevations as one of the numerous springs.

Nearby is a roadside sign describing the "Big lime of the driller." This refers to the thick limestones of the Greenbrier formation of Mississippian age. Drillers like the Greenbrier because oil and gas are often found in this formation where it is covered by younger rocks and found far underground. Cave explorers like the Greenbrier because numerous caves, including some of the largest in the state, are found in this formation when it is close to the surface. Here and elsewhere in eastern West Virginia, the Greenbrier formation forms the gray pavement-like outcrops that you see.

WV 3 leads you through two gaps in the low hills. Between the two is a road on the left leading in a few miles to Moncove Lake State Park. The park offers fishing, boating, hiking, camping, and picnicking at a secluded lake.

Past the second gap is the town of Gap Mills. Once known for the several water-powered mills that operated here, the town is now home to several craft and specialty shops. Continue on WV 3, which turns northeast (left). You are now in the broad, open farmlands of Sweet Springs Valley, with the long ridge of Peters Mountain to the right.

The Appalachian Trail winds along this ridgeline at the western edge of the Jefferson National Forest, and in most places it marks the boundary between Virginia and West Virginia. The Hanging Rock Observatory at the top of the ridge in a former fire tower is known for its studies of hawk migration.

The drive gradually climbs until it reaches the Great Eastern Divide. Ahead, the streams flow eventually into the James River and Chesapeake Bay. Behind, where you have been driving all day, the water flows into the New River, and eventually the Ohio and Mississippi Rivers.

A few miles farther is the former Sweet Springs Hotel, which in its heyday was one of the largest. The original hotel was built in 1792; the present brick-columnar structure was constructed in 1833 based on a design by Thomas Jefferson. Presidential guests included George Washington and Franklin Pierce. The property was saved from destruction when it was bought by the state of West Virginia in 1945 and used as a tuberculosis sanitarium and later as a home for the aged. Springs still bubble and gurgle in the open center of the brick bathhouse; the water has been bottled and sold and is known for its "acidic briskness."

The drive ends here, about 1 mile from the Virginia line. You can retrace the drive, or continue straight ahead on VA 311. Just past the state boundary is Sweet Chalybeate Springs, where you can see a pool, small waterfall, and gazebo. "Chalybeate" means "tasting like iron." The spring is also known as Red Sweet Springs. From there, you can continue on curvy VA 311, which intersects with I–64/US 60 a few miles south of White Sulphur Springs.

23

coal Heritage Trail

BLUEFIELD TO BECKLEY

GENERAL DESCRIPTION: A 97-mile, winding drive from Bluefield to Beckley through the heart of coal country past mining camps and owners' mansion, mines, tipples, and company stores.

SPECIAL ATTRACTIONS: Pinnacle Rock, Bramwell, coal mining camps and equipment, and Beckley Exhibition Coal Mine.

LOCATION: Southern West Virginia.

DRIVING ROUTE NUMBERS AND NAME: US 19, 52; WV 16.

TRAVEL SEASON: All year.

CAMPING: Twin Falls State Park has fifty campsites, most with hookups, and is open during the warmer months. Camp Creek State Park has thirty-six tent/trailer sites. Beckley has several private campgrounds.

SERVICES: All services are plentiful in Bluefield and Beckley. Gas and food are available in most towns along the drive.

NEARBY ATTRACTIONS: New River Gorge, Tamarack, outdoor dramas, Twin Falls State Park, Grandview, Beckley Exhibition Coal Mine, and Pocahontas (Virginia) Exhibition Mine.

THE DRIVE

The ancient Greeks called it "the rock that burns." Halfway around the world from Greece and hundreds of millions of years ago huge swamps and marshes repeatedly covered much of what is now West Virginia. The organic material in the swamps was buried and compacted as thousands of feet of other sediments were deposited on top of it. Eventually it was converted into a soft black rock with a high percentage of carbon—coal, the rock that powered the modernization of the United States and transformed West Virginia from a wilderness into a vital industrial center.

In the 1870s the Norfolk and Western (N&W) and the Chesapeake and Ohio (C&O) railroads reached the huge coalfields of southern West Virginia. Almost overnight, communities grew into blossoming boom towns, and the fortunate mine owners found themselves to be new millionaires.

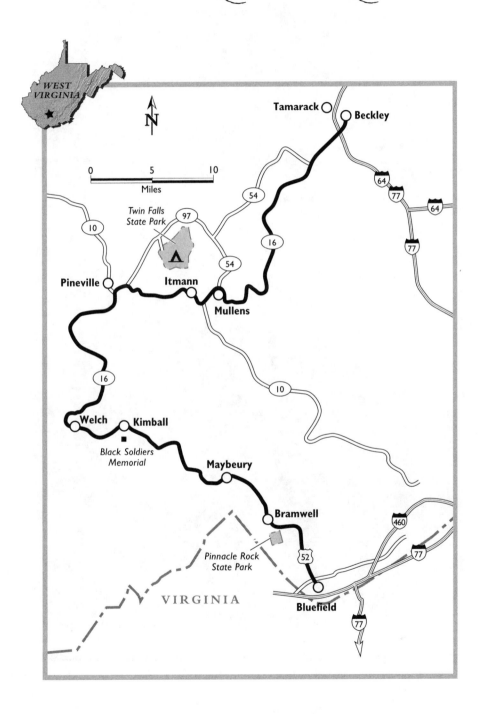

Pinnacle Rock looms over the picnic area.

This 97-mile drive passes through the heart of coal country in southern West Virginia. You'll see the ornate mansions of the mine owners and row after row of miners' houses. You'll also see company stores, mines, coal tipples, huge railroad yards, and narrow stream valleys. The drive is entirely on two-lane, paved roads that are often used by coal trucks.

Bluefield straddles the Virginia–West Virginia border near the center of the famed Pocahontas Coalfield. Pocahontas coal—low in sulfur, high in carbon—became the standard by which all other bituminous coal was measured. Worldwide it helped power the Industrial Revolution, and it drove U.S. Navy ships in both World War I and the Spanish American War. Rail fans will want to visit the extensive railroad yards, which featured "natural gravity" loading. Bluefield flourished as the de facto capital of the southern West Virginia and Virginia coalfields from 1900 to the 1920s.

The elegant Old City Hall, built in a classical revival style, is home to the Science Center of West Virginia, an art gallery, and a theater. It's also the starting point for a walking tour of other historical buildings. Nearby is the Eastern Regional Coal Archives, with an extensive collection of coal mining material, from miners' tools to old photographs to company records and correspondence.

East River Mountain dominates the city's skyline along the boundary between Virginia and West Virginia. If you have the time, drive to the East River Mountain Scenic Overlook (take WV 598 off US 460) for a bird's-eye view of the city and surrounding mountains from 3,500 feet. This is also the midpoint of a loop drive between Bluefield and Wytheville, Virginia; that drive, "Over and Under Big Walker" is described in The Globe Pequot Press' FalconGuide *Scenic Driving Virginia*.

To begin this drive go west on US 52. After a few strip malls, you're out in hilly country and soon come to Pinnacle Rock State Park. This wayside park has nothing to do with coal, but it has commanding views from the top of this huge slab of sandstone and is a pleasant place to picnic.

About 5 miles from Bluefield is the turnoff for Bramwell (pronounced to rhyme with "camel"), once considered the richest town in the United States. Settled by mine-owner barons in the early 1900s, the town was home to as many as nineteen new millionaires made wealthy by the underground toils of others. In the early 1900s they built elegant and opulent Victorian-style mansions with copper roofs, inlaid Italian marble stonework, and even an indoor swimming pool.

BRAMWELL, RICHEST TOWN IN THE COUNTRY

The aristocratic residents enjoyed an active social life, but if life in town grew boring, fourteen trains per day stopped at the town station, including three to New York. The tiny Bank of Bramwell had the highest deposits per capita of any bank in the country; with all that money entrusted to it, it financed projects far from its doors, including the prestigious Burning Tree Country Club outside Washington, D.C.

Of course, you already know what happened to millionaires in 1929. As the stock market crashed, so did their fortunes. But the buildings remained, nearly all of them well preserved today. In 1983 the entire town was placed on the National Register of Historic Places. Several of the mansions have been refurbished as bed-and-breakfast inns. The restored train station is now a visitor center where you can plan pick up a tour guide and plan your visit. Several times a year the Bramwell Millionaire Garden Club conducts guided tours through the town.

Past Bramwell on US 52 the valleys narrow and the hills become closer and steeper. At roadcuts look for black seams of coal in the flat-lying rocks.

The mine owners in Bramwell lived in fine mansions like this.

Miners lived in less opulent housing, as shown in this 1920s photo.
Photo: Courtesy West Virginia State Archives.

The road passes through small mining camps such as Elkhorn, with company housing, the railroad, a coal-loading tipple, and a small stream strung out along the road.

More than 100,000 miners toiled in West Virginia's coalfields during the boom years. Miners came from all over the world, including black Americans fleeing the Deep South and Eastern European immigrants seeking a better life in the New World. A hundred years ago coal mining was laborious, dark, and dangerous hand work. Highly mechanized and technologically sophisticated today, the coal industry produces more coal than ever with fewer miners. Some 500 small company camps have been recognized along the Coal Heritage Trail, many of them just remnants of their former glory. Isolated as they were, miners were united by family, church, and community, with scant attention paid to racial or ethnic differences.

WORLD WAR I BLACK SOLDIERS MEMORIAL

At Kimball is the World War I Black Soldiers Memorial, the only such memorial in the country. Unfortunately fire damaged much of the building several years ago, but restoration is underway. Also in Kimball and undergoing renovation is the McDowell County Coal Heritage Museum, in a former coal company store.

At the center of town in Welch you can't miss the McDowell County Court House, with its three-story clock tower. Built in 1894, this imposing Romanesque Revival structure is best known as the site of a shootout in 1921, when union organizer Sid Hatfield and another man were killed by coal company detectives. (See Drive 20, Hatfield–McCoy Country, for more about this incident.)

Turn north (right) on WV 16 in Welch. This road has less traffic and fewer towns than the first part of the drive. The road is less curvy but more up and down. After Pineville, look for reclaimed land and treeless valleys from former mines.

By the highway in Itmann (named for Bramwell banker Isaac. T. Mann) is a huge and ornate company store once operated by the Pocahontas Fuel Company. Much smaller are the prefab miners' homes, built in 1916 but still occupied.

More spacious and up-to-date is Twin Falls State Park, north of this drive near Mullens, which features a resort lodge and eighteen-hole champion golf course. One of the nine hiking trails leads past the namesake waterfalls. A campground is open from Easter through October.

Miners with large families would find the tiny coal camp houses in Black Eagle cramped. Be sure to notice the huge reclaimed coalfield as the road climbs the long slope after crossing the railroad tracks in Ury.

From here WV 16 continues for another 14 miles past more coal camps to exit 42 of I–64/77 and the end of the drive at Beckley. You may want to cap off your drive with a tour of the Beckley Exhibition Mine or a visit to Tamarack, the state's showcase for the arts and crafts. Beckley is also the gateway for excursions into the New River Gorge. For a fast trip back to Bluefield, take I–77 south.

24

The Best of the Midland Trail

OLD US 60

GENERAL DESCRIPTION: An 81-mile drive on US 60 over the northern two-thirds of the Midland Trail Scenic Highway from Sam Black Church to Malden, past historical sights, views of the New River Gorge, and the Kanawha River.

SPECIAL ATTRACTIONS: Meadow River Wildlife Management Area, Babcock and Hawks Nest State Parks, New River Gorge National River, Kanawha and Cathedral Falls, Cabin Creek Quilts, and African Zion Baptist Church.

LOCATION: South-central West Virginia.

DRIVING ROUTE NUMBERS AND NAME: US 60, the Midland Trail.

TRAVEL SEASON: All year.

CAMPING: Babcock State Park has fifty-one sites, most with hookups. Private campgrounds are numerous, located near White Sulphur Springs, Hico, Glen Jean, and Fayetteville.

SERVICES: All services are available along the drive.

NEARBY ATTRACTIONS: The Greenbrier resort, Lewisburg, Lost World Caverns, Organ Cave, New River Gorge National River, Gauley River National Recreation Area, Carnifex Ferry Battlefield State Park, and Charleston.

THE DRIVE

The Midland Trail Scenic Highway follows US 60 from the Virginia border to Charleston. Once part of the main transcontinental highway system, US 60 became a secondary route for local traffic after completion of I–64 in 1988.

This route has been important for centuries, first as a buffalo trail and American Indian footpath. By the 1750s European settlers used the trail to reach the western frontiers. George Washington, Daniel Boone, Daniel Webster, Henry Clay, Andrew Jackson, Rutherford B. Hayes, and William McKinley have traversed it.

THE BEST OF THE MIDLAND TRAIL

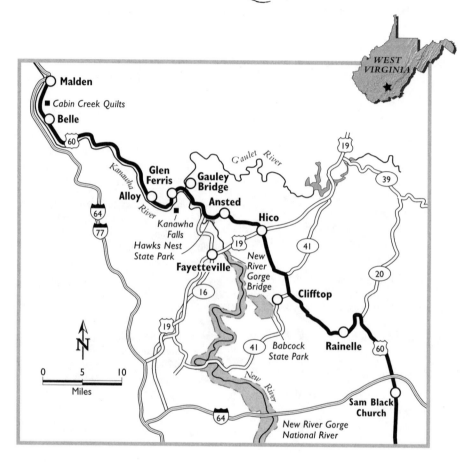

In 1824 the road was improved and renamed the Kanawha Turnpike and later extended to Charleston and Kentucky. Coaches carried passengers, mail, and freight. With completion of the C&O Railroad in 1873, the road's importance decreased. Years later as automobiles become commonplace, the road, now called the Midland Trail, became part of the first transcontinental route. In 1924 national highways were designated and assigned numbers, and the Midland Trail became "Route 60." For more than six decades US 60 was a vital link in the transcontinental highway system, as cars, trucks, freight, and passengers passed back and forth over its scenic and historic terrain.

When I–64 was completed in 1988, US 60 again became a secondary road for local traffic. After years of neglect, US 60 today has been restored to its rightful place in history and designated the Midland Trail Scenic Highway.

Brown markers display the miles along the route, starting at mile 0 at the State Capitol in Charleston south to mile 123 at the Virginia border in White Sulphur Springs. Most pioneers and early settlers followed the trail north from Virginia, and that is how it is described here. You can, of course, do the ride in either direction.

Described here are 81 miles of the Trail from Sam Black Church at exit 156 of I–64 at mile 85 of the Midland Trail, ending at Malden, just off exit 96 of I–64/77, at mile 4.

For a longer ride you can begin on US 60 at mile 119 near the Virginia border at White Sulphur Springs, home of the famed Greenbrier resort. This section parallels I–64, crossing it several times, and provides a less-traveled, two-lane, bucolic alternative to the interstate, through Lewisburg and the rolling "Big Meadows" farmlands in the fertile limestone cavernous valleys. It's worth the trip, but because most of this area is well described in Drives 18 (Greenbrier River Valley) and 21 (Athens to Lewisburg), it's not described in detail here.

Start at Sam Black Church. The actual church is south of the interstate interchange. The Reverend Sam Black, a Methodist circuit rider for many years in the late 1800s, preached at this church.

From the church go north on US 60. At mile 83 look for the sign pointing left to Meadow River Wildlife Management Area. During the spring and fall migrations, this large wetlands is an important stop for waterfowl, including mallards, teals, and wood ducks. In spring listen for the call of several species of frogs, including spring peepers, bull frogs, pickerel frogs, and green frogs.

The long uphill stretch past Rainelle winds up the slopes of Sewell Mountain. Imagine yourself a hundred years ago climbing this hill by foot, horseback, or stagecoach on a steamy summer's day, perhaps even driving a herd of sheep or cattle.

BABCOCK STATE PARK

At Clifftop, just past mile 63, WV 41 goes left 4 miles to Babcock State Park near the edge of the New River Gorge. Its 20 miles of hiking trails lead to numerous overlooks into the New River Gorge National River. At the restored and frequently photographed Glade Creek Grist Mill, you can watch the waterwheel turn and buy freshly ground corn meal.

Visitors examine the waterwheel at Glade Creek Grist Mill in Babcock State Park.

Nearby is Camp Washington–Carver, better known to fans of old-time music as Clifftop. Originally built as the nation's first black 4-H camp by the Civilian Conservation Corps, the state-run site features several music festivals including folk, do-wop, and classic rock and roll.

Back on the Trail, you pass Spy Rock, a favorite spot of early native Americans, used as an observation station during the Civil War. At mile 57 the drive passes through the town of Lookout, the start of Drive 17, which descends into the New River Gorge National River. At Hico, mile 53, is the intersection with US 19; a few miles south on US 19 is the dramatic conclusion to Drive 17 at the Canyon Rim Visitor Center and the New River Gorge Bridge.

On the other side of Amsted, at mile 45, be sure to stop, even if only briefly, at Hawks Nest State Park, perched on the rim of the New River Gorge. A tramway descends into the gorge where you can take a jet boat ride upstream almost to the base of the New River Gorge Bridge, 976 feet above the water, during the warmer months. Those feeling more energetic can follow several trails along the rim or to the bottom of the gorge. The lodge and restaurant allow you to watch the sunset over the New River from your table or room. To the right along the river is a large dam and hydroelectric plant.

From Hawks Nest, the drive slowly descends to river level, with several scenic turnouts on the way down. At Gauley Bridge, mile 38, the New and the Gauley Rivers emerge from their white-water gorges and unite to form the wide Kanawha River, which you will follow for the rest of the drive.

At Glen Ferris is the historic Glen Ferris Inn. Opened in 1836 as the Stockton Inn to service travelers on the old Kanawha Turnpike, it continues operations today. The Federal-style inn overlooks the gentle Kanawha Falls spanning the river; a small park near the falls is a favorite fishing and picnic area.

About 1 mile from Glen Ferris on the right is smaller and cozier Cathedral Falls, which tumbles over moss-covered rocks to a room-like enclosure at the base. In winter the frozen falls form a glistening cascade of crystal ice.

The drive continues downstream along the broad flood plain, becoming increasingly more urbanized and industrial. The road is level, with no major curves. At mile 31 in Alloy is a modern ferro-alloy plant. Many of the small towns are former coal camps, some still active, including two working mines and processing plants whose conveyers cross the highway and can be seen extending up into the neighboring bluffs.

In 1938 the U.S. Army Corps of Engineers built a series of lock and dams along the Kanawha to smooth out the 9-foot drop between Kanawha Falls and Charleston. The easiest one to visit is at London, mile 24.

Folks fish and relax at Kanawha Falls.

The Best of the Midland Trail

Booker T. Washington worshipped and was married at the African Zion Baptist Church in Malden.

West of Belle US 60 becomes a four-lane highway. You can continue along the Midland Trail on the old road, which parallels the highway, to Malden, mile 4.

BOOKER T. WASHINGTON AND CABIN CREEK QUILTS

Malden is best known today as the home of Cabin Creek Quilts, a cooperative of more than 300 quilters and other artisans. Their arts are displayed in the 1838 Hale House on the north end of town. In addition to exquisite quilts, you can admire and buy wall hangings, aprons, placemats, skirts, and other clothing, and even Christmas decorations and coffee mugs.

During the nineteenth century Malden was the center of the booming salt industry and known as Kanawha Salines. Before the Civil War slaves carried out much of the salt manufacturing; after the war many of them remained here as free men. They worshipped in the African Zion Baptist Church, founded in 1863. The present graceful plain frame church, near Cabin Creek Quilts, was built in 1872 and is on the National Register of Historic Places.

The most famous member of this congregation is the black educator, Booker T. Washington. Born in Virginia, he came to Malden when he was nine years old when his family was freed after the Civil War. After attending Hampton Institute, Washington returned to Malden, where he married and served as schoolmaster, leaving several years later to become headmaster of the Tuskegee Institute in Alabama. His home is no longer standing, but a small public park and monument honor him here. Washington's groundbreaking book, *Up from Slavery*, describes his life in Malden.

The drive ends here at Malden near Exit 96 of I–64/77. You can also continue on US 60 and the Midland Scenic Trail into Charleston to the state capitol.

SOURCES OF
MORE INFORMATION

For more information on lands and events, please
contact the following agencies and organizations.

GENERAL INFORMATION

West Virginia Division of Tourism
2101 Washington Street, E
Charleston, WV 25305
800 CALL WVA (800–225–5982)
www.callwva.com

The West Virginia Division of Tourism provides exemplary services for visitors and prospective visitors. Call them for information or to be directly connected toll free with any state agency, including parks, forests, and wildlife management areas plus many privately owned facilities.

They will also help you plan your trip, answer questions, and provide maps and phone numbers. Do you want a list of rafting companies, the best time to see the autumn leaves at the New River Gorge, or when the Feast of Ramson will be held in Richfield? Contact them by phone, fax, e-mail, or regular mail, and they will send you a list, a map, or just give you the information. You can also use the travel planner on the state's Web site.

DRIVE 1
NORTHERN PANHANDLE

HISTORIC BETHANY
Bethany College
Bethany, WV 26032
304–829–7285
historic@mail.bethanywv.edu
www.bethanywv.edu

OGLEBAY RESORT AND CONFERENCE CENTER
Route 88 N.
Wheeling, WV 26003
800–624–6988
304–243–4000

WHEELING WEST VIRGINIA CONVENTION AND VISITORS BUREAU
1401 Main Street
Wheeling, WV 26003
800–828–3097
304–233–7709
info@wheelingcvb.com
www.wheelingcvb.com

WEIRTON CHAMBER OF COMMERCE
3147 West Street
Weirton, WV 26062
304–748–7212

DRIVE 2
MOUNDSVILLE TO FAIRMONT

GRAVE CREEK MOUND HISTORIC SITE
801 Jefferson Avenue
Moundsville, WV 26041
304–843–4128

MARION COUNTY CONVENTION AND VISITORS BUREAU
110 Adams Street
Fairmont, WV 26554
800–834–7365
304–368–1123
www.marioncvb.co,

PALACE OF GOLD
RD 1 NBU #24
Moundsville, WV 26041
304–843–1812
newvrindaban@yahoo.com
www.palaceofgold.com

WEST AUGUSTA HISTORICAL SOCIETY
P.O. Box 414
Mannington, WV 26582
304–986–2636
304–986–1298

WEST VIRGINIA STATE PENITENTIARY TOURS
818 Jefferson Avenue
Moundsville, VA 26041
304–845–6200
www.wvpentours.com

DRIVE 3
ALONG THE OHIO RIVER

**BLENNERHASSETT ISLAND
HISTORICAL STATE PARK**
137 Juliana Street
Parkersburg, WV 26101-5331
304–420–4800 Museum

**NEW MARTINSVILLE CHAMBER
OF COMMERCE**
200 Main Street
P.O. Box 271
New Martinsville, WV 26155
304–455–3825
www.twinbridges.com

**OHIO RIVER ISLANDS
NATIONAL WILDLIFE REFUGE**
3004 7th Street
P.O. Box 1811
Parkersburg, WV 26102
304–422–0752

OIL AND GAS MUSEUM
P.O. Box 1685
Parkersburg, WV 26102
304–485–5446

**PARKERSBURG/WOOD COUNTY
CONVENTION AND VISITORS
BUREAU**
350 7th Street
Parkersburg, WV 26101
304–428–1130
800–752–4982
info@parkersburgcvb.org
www.parkersburgcvb.com

SISTERSVILLE CITY HALL
200 Diamond Street
Sistersville, WV 26175
304–652–6361

DRIVE 4
**KINGWOOD TO CATHEDRAL
STATE PARK**

CATHEDRAL STATE PARK
Route 1 Box 370
Aurora, WV 26705
304–735–3771
www.wvparks.com/cathedral

**PRESTON COUNTY
CONVENTION AND VISITORS
BUREAU**
P.O. Box 860
Arthurdale, WV 26520
304–864–4601
800–571–0912
prestoncvb@prestoncounty.com
www.prestoncounty.com

DRIVE 5
ROMNEY-KEYSER LOOP

FORT ASHBY
P.O. Box 233
Fort Ashby, WV 26719
304–298–3319

POTOMAC EAGLE RAILROAD
P.O. Box 657 Route 28
Romney, WV 26757
800–22–EAGLE

DRIVE 6
BERKELEY SPRINGS TO PAW PAW

BERKELEY SPRINGS STATE PARK
121 South Washington Street
Berkeley Springs, WV 25411
304–258–5860
www.berkeleysprings.com

CHESAPEAKE AND OHIO CANAL NATIONAL HISTORIC PARK
Hancock Visitor Center
326 E. Main Street
Hancock, MD 21750
301–678–5463

TRAVEL BERKELEY SPRINGS
304 Fairfax Street
Berkeley Springs, WV 25411
800–447–8797
tbs@intrepid.net
www.berkeleysprings.com

DRIVE 7
HISTORIC EASTERN PANHANDLE

JEFFERSON COUNTY CONVENTION AND VISITORS BUREAU
P.O. Box A
Harpers Ferry, WV 25425
304–535–2627
800–848–TOUR
visitors@jeffersoncountycvb.com

MARTINSBURG/BERKELEY COUNTY CONVENTION AND VISITORS BUREAU
208 South Queen Street
Martinsburg, WV 25401
304–264–8801
800–498–2386
boconnor@travelwv.com

RUMSEY STEAMBOAT MUSEUM
c/o O'Hurley's General Store
Shepherdstown, WV 25443
304–876–6907

HARPERS FERRY NATIONAL HISTORIC PARK
P.O. Box 65
Harpers Ferry, WV 25425
304–535–6298

DRIVE 8
CENTER STATE RAMBLE

BUCKHANNON/UPSHUR CHAMBER OF COMMERCE
16 S. Kanawha Street
P.O. Box 442
Buckhannon, WV 26201
304–472–1722
cocoltchos@mountain.net

PHILIPPI CONVENTION AND VISITOR BUREAU
124 Main Street
Philippi, WV 26416
304–457–3700 ext. 211

SWISS VILLAGE OF HELVETIA
Helvetia WV 26224
304–924–6435

WEST VIRGINIA WILDLIFE
CENTER
P.O. Box 38
French Creek, WV 26218
304–924–6211

DRIVE 9
CANAAN VALLEY LOOP

BLACKWATER FALLS STATE PARK
P.O. Drawer 490
Davis, WV 26260
304–259–5216
800–225–5982
blackwatr@access.mountain.net
wvweb.com

CANAAN VALLEY NATIONAL
WILDLIFE REFUGE
P.O. Box 1278
Elkins, WV 26241
304–637–7312

CANAAN VALLEY RESORT &
CONFERENCE CENTER AND
CANAAN VALLEY
HC 70, Box 330
Davis, WV 26260
304–866–4121
800–622–4121
www.canaanresort.com

DRIVE 10
THROUGH GREENLAND GAP

HARDY COUNTY HISTORICAL
SOCIETY
111 North Main Street
Moorefield, WV 26836

THE NATURE CONSERVANCY
West Virginia Chapter
304–345–4530

DRIVE 11
LOST RIVER AND CACAPON RIVER

LOST RIVER STATE PARK
HC 67, Box 24
Mathias, WV 26812
304–897–5372
800–225–5982
www.lostriversp.com

DRIVE 12
DOLLY SODS SCENIC AREA

USDA FOREST SERVICE
MONONGAHELA NATIONAL
FOREST
Forest Headquarters
200 Sycamore Street
Elkins, WV 26241
304–636–1800

USDA FOREST SERVICE
MONONGAHELA NATIONAL
FOREST
Seneca Rocks Visitor Center
P.O. Box 13
Seneca Rocks, WV 26884
304–567–2827

DRIVE 13
POTOMAC HIGHLANDS LOOP

USDA FOREST SERVICE
MONONGAHELA NATIONAL
FOREST
Forest Headquarters
200 Sycamore Street
Elkins, WV 26241
304–636–1800

USDA FOREST SERVICE
MONONGAHELA NATIONAL
FOREST
Seneca Rocks Visitor Center
P.O. Box 13
Seneca Rocks, WV 26884
304–567–2827

DRIVE 14
**SPRUCE KNOB AND SPRUCE
KNOB LAKE**

USDA FOREST SERVICE
MONONGAHELA NATIONAL
FOREST
Forest Headquarters
200 Sycamore Street
Elkins, WV 26241
304–636–1800

USDA FOREST SERVICE
MONONGAHELA NATIONAL
FOREST
Seneca Rocks Visitor Center
P.O. Box 13
Seneca Rocks, WV 26884
304–567–2827

DRIVE 15
HIGHLAND SCENIC HIGHWAY

MONONGAHELA NATIONAL
FOREST
MARLINTON RANGER DISTRICT
P.O. Box 210
Marlinton, WV 24954
304–799–4334

MONONGAHELA NATIONAL
FOREST
Gauley Ranger District
P.O. Box 110
Richwood, WV 26261
304–846–2695

RICHWOOD AREA CHAMBER OF
COMMERCE
P.O. Box 267
Richwood, WV 26261
304–846–6790

WEST VIRGINIA RAILS-TO-
TRAILS COUNCIL FOR
CRANBERRY TRI-RIVER RAIL
TRAIL
P.O. Box 8889
South Charleston, WV 25303

DRIVE 16
RAILROAD LOOP AND THE NATIONAL RADIO ASTRONOMY OBSERVATORY

CASS SCENIC RAILROAD STATE PARK
P.O. Box 107 Route 66
Cass, WV 24927
304–456–4300
www.neumedia.net/~cassrr/

DURBIN AND GREENBRIER VALLEY RAILROAD
P.O. Box 44
Durbin, WV 26264
304–456–4935
877–686–7245

NATIONAL RADIO ASTRONOMY OBSERVATORY
P.O. Box 2
Green Bank, WV 24944
304–456–2011
www.nrao.edu

SNOWSHOE MOUNTAIN RESORT
10 Snowshoe Drive
Snowshoe, WV 26209
304–572–1000
www.snowshoemtn.com

DRIVE 17
NEW RIVER GORGE AND BRIDGE

AFRICAN-AMERICAN HERITAGE FAMILY TREE MUSEUM
HC 67, Box 58
Ansted, WV 25812
304–658–5889
304–658–5526

FAYETTEVILLE VISITORS CENTER
120 Windsor Lane
Fayetteville, WV 25840
888–574–1500

NATIONAL PARK SERVICE NEW RIVER GORGE NATIONAL RIVER
Canyon Rim Visitor Center
P.O. Box 246
Glen Jean, WV 25846-0246
304–574–2115
neri_interpretation@nps.gov
www.nps.gov/neri

NATIONAL PARK SERVICE NEW RIVER GORGE NATIONAL RIVER
Headquarters
P.O. Box 246
Glen Jean, WV 25846
304–574–2115

DRIVE 18
GREENBRIER RIVER VALLEY

BEARTOWN AND DROOP MOUNTAIN BATTLEFIELD STATE PARKS
HC 64 Box 189
Hillsboro WV 24946
304–653–4254
www.wvparks.com/droopmountain
battlefield

WATOGA STATE PARK AND THE GREENBRIER RIVER TRAIL
HC 82, Box 252
Marlinton, WV 24954
304–799–4087
800–CALL–WVA
www.watoga.com

LEWISBURG VISITORS CENTER
105 Church Street
Lewisburg, WV 24901
800–833–2068
304–645–1000

LOST WORLD CAVERNS
Route 6, Box 308
Lewisburg, WV 24901
304–645–6677
wildcaveman@hotmail.com

MONONGAHELA NATIONAL FOREST
Marlinton Ranger District
P.O. Box 210
Marlinton, WV 24954
304–799–4334

POCAHONTAS COUNTY TOURISM COMMISSION
P.O. Box 275
Marlinton, WV 24954
304–799–4636
www.pocahontas.org

DRIVE 19
THURMOND DEPOT

NATIONAL PARK SERVICE
New River Gorge National River
Headquarters
P.O. Box 246
Glen Jean, WV 25846
304–465–0508

THURMOND DEPOT VISITOR CENTER
304–465–8550 seasonally
www.nps.gov/neri

NEW RIVER TRAIN EXCURSIONS
Collis P. Huntington RR Historical
Society
1429 Chestnut Street
Kenova, WV 25530-1235
606–325–8800

DRIVE 20
HATFIELD-MCCOY COUNTRY

MATEWAN DEVELOPMENT CENTER, INC.
P.O. Box 368
Matewan, WV 25678
304–426–4239
matewan@eastky.net

TUG VALLEY CHAMBER OF
COMMERCE COAL HOUSE
2nd Avenue and Court Street
P.O. Box 376
Williamson, WV 25661
304–235–5240

DRIVE 21
ATHENS TO LEWISBURG

BLUESTONE DAM
U.S. Army Corps of Engineers
701 Miller Avenue
Hinton, WV 25951
304–466–1234
davide@lrh.usace.army.mil

BLUESTONE STATE PARK
HC 78 Box 3
Hinton, WV 25951
304–466–2805
800–225–5982
bluestonestatepark@citynet.net
www.bluestonesp.com

LEWISBURG VISITORS CENTER
105 Church Street
Lewisburg, WV 24901
800–833–2068
304–645–1000

ORGAN CAVE
417 Masters Road
Ronceverte, WV 24970
304–645–7600

PENCE SPRINGS HOTEL
P.O. Box 90
Pence Springs, WV 24962
304–445–2606
800–826–1829
pencehotel@newwave.net

PIPESTEM RESORT STATE PARK
Route 20, P.O. Box 150
Pipestem, WV 25979
304–466–1800
800–225–5982
pipestem@cwv.net
www.pipestemresort.com

DRIVE 22
**FARM HERITAGE ROAD SCENIC
BYWAY**

MONROE COUNTY HISTORICAL
SOCIETY AND TOURIST
INFORMATION CENTER
P.O. Box 24
Union, WV 24983
304–772–3003
304–832–6326

DRIVE 23
COAL HERITAGE TRAIL

BLUESTONE CONVENTION AND
VISITORS BUREAU
500 Bland Street
Bluefield, WV 24701
304–325–8438
800–221–3206

CITY OF WELCH
Welch Municipal Building
88 Howard Street
Welch, WV 24801
304–436–3113

COAL HERITAGE TRAIL ASSOCIATION
City Hall
Bramwell, WV 24715
800–248–1866

SOUTHERN WEST VIRGINIA CONVENTION AND VISITORS BUREAU
511 Ewart Avenue
P.O. Box 1799
Beckley, WV 25801
304–252–2244
800–VISIT–WV
travel@visitwv.org
www.visitwv.org

TAMARACK
One Tamarack Drive
Beckley, WV 25801
304–256–6843

TWIN FALLS RESORT STATE PARK
Route 97, Box 1023
Mullens, WV 25882
304–294–4000
800–CALL–WVA

DRIVE 24
THE BEST OF THE MIDLAND TRAIL

CABIN CREEK QUILTS
4208 Malden Drive
Malden, WV 23506
304–925–9499

MIDLAND TRAIL SCENIC HIGHWAY ASSOCIATION
P.O. Box 60061
Malden, WV 25306
800–CALL–WVA
www.wvmidlandtrail.com/

HAWKS NEST STATE PARK
P.O. Box 857
Ansted, WV 25812
304–658–5212
800–CALL–WVA
hawksnest@citynet.net

BABCOCK STATE PARK
HC 35, Box 150
Clifftop, WV 25831
304–438–3004
800–CALL–WVA
babcock@mail.wvnet.edu

Index

O

P

R

S

About the Author

Bruce Sloane has been a geologist, park ranger, newspaper editor, author, humor columnist, and technical writer. He writes about travel, the natural world, and history, and lives in the Blue Ridge Mountains of Virginia, where on clear days he can see West Virginia. His wife, Joy Sloane, accompanies him on his travels to make sure he does not forget the film, maps, or his toothbrush. Bruce is the author of *Scenic Driving Virginia* and two other books. He holds bachelor and master's degrees in geology.